Theodore F Price

**Songs of the Southwest**

Theodore F Price

**Songs of the Southwest**

ISBN/EAN: 9783743329041

Manufactured in Europe, USA, Canada, Australia, Japa

Cover: Foto ©ninafisch / pixelio.de

Manufactured and distributed by brebook publishing software (www.brebook.com)

Theodore F Price

**Songs of the Southwest**

# SONGS

## OF THE

# SOUTHWEST.

# Songs of the Southwest;

BY

THEODORE F. PRICE,

THE DRAMATIC IMPERSONATOR.

TOPEKA, KANSAS:
GEO. W. CRANE & CO., PUBLISHERS,
1881.

Copyright applied for.

TO PROFESSOR DAVID SWING,

OF CHICAGO.

# CONTENTS:

|  | PAGE. |
|---|---|
| THE VALLEY OF THE ARKANSAS, | 1 |
| LEDFORD'S LEAGUE, | 12 |
| A PRAIRIE ROMANCE, | 27 |
| HANK HAWKINS, THE SHOWMAN, | 37 |
| THE PRAIRIE FIRE, | 49 |
| THE CARNIVAL OF DEATH, | 59 |
| LORA, | 79 |
| FRAGMENTS FROM NEWTON: | |
|     The Coachman of the Mountains, | 89 |
|     Marshal King, | 93 |
|     Ruin, | 97 |
|     The Scorge of Locusts, | 101 |
|     Dawning Day, | 103 |
| DEATH OF PRESIDENT LINCOLN, | 107 |
| THE SIEGE, | 113 |
| CHARGE OF THE ICONOCLAST, | 123 |
| MISCELLANEOUS: | |
|     Night Scene on the Mississippi, | 135 |
|     Tennyson, | 141 |
|     Bryant, | 143 |
|     Unrest, | 145 |
|     Geese, | 147 |
|     The Haunted Soul, | 153 |
|     The Festival Fills Me with Sadness, | 157 |
|     The Soul's Mirror, | 159 |
|     To H*****, | 163 |
|     Oh! Gently Blow, ye Autumn Gales! | 165 |
|     Remorse, | 167 |
|     Your Sister, | 169 |
|     She Lives Again, | 171 |
|     Earlham College Games, | 173 |
|     The Auctioneer, | 177 |
|     To Leona, | 183 |
|     The Poachers' Defeat, | 185 |
|     To Miss A*** B*****, | 189 |

*A voice of music, like a singing bee,—*
   *Lone on the prairie, on the mountain brown,*
   *On mighty rivers, in the midnight town—*
*Delights my ear, and bears me company;*
   *Breathing strange legends of the vale and wood;*
   *Bidding me peer where fiery passions brood;—*
*Paints pictures on my soul of all I see,*
*And syllables harmonious thoughts to me.*
   *Delightful spirit of my solitude!*
*When mind lay fettered with its heavy chain,*
   *Thou with bright hope my darkest hour imbued;*
*My harp, re-strung, thou gave to me again;—*
*Hark! the faint echo, stealing on the ear!*
*Far off, and faint—the light vibrations hear!*

CHICAGO, DECEMBER 21, 1876.

# THE VALLEY

# OF THE ARKANSAS.

# Songs of the Southwest.

## THE VALLEY OF THE ARKANSAS.

A STREAM flows winding through the West,
From Colorado's canyon's deep;
Far springing from her mountain crest,
The waters wild in torrents leap
To quench the thirst of burning sands,
Then glow anon mid verdant lands.

All treeless lie, on either side,
The shores for many a trackless league;
No landmark looms the way to guide,
Save yonder far off mountain peak,
Where sage with spiny cactus grows,
Nor bough a grateful shadow throws.

The plainsman with his weary train
Long days has journeyed, parched with thirst;
Then, gleaming far along the plain,
Those wished-for waters cheering burst

On his glad vision—lifted high
Like molten silver 'gainst the sky.

Brown herds of lordly buffalo,
Wild dromedaries of the plain,
Surge restlessly as ocean's flow,
Far grazing o'er the grassy main—
Then starting up in wild affright,
Wake jarring thunders in their flight!

Their deadly enemy appears,
Whose near approach some ruse beguiled—
No mustang troop the bison fears;
He scents the huntsman of the wild,
By mane and neck almost concealed,
Crest scarcely o'er the steed revealed.

Then firmly grasping bow and spear,
Along his charger's neck inclined,
The savage speeds in mad career
With scalp-lock streaming in the wind;
His hapless victim singled out
From 'mong the panic-stricken rout.

Urged from the borders of his troop,
The bison vainly strives to flee;

Then veering like the vulture's swoop,
The foe pursues relentlessly;
The pond'rous prey with horns held low
Charges, enraged, the agile foe.

Still close beside the huntsmen ride,
Hoarse bellowings speak the bison's pain;
The arrows gash his gory side,
Their feathered shafts are in his mane—
The lance gleams through the savage sport—
A heavy fall—a dying snort.

The squaw will strip the smoking hide,
The hump regale the stalwart brave;
The gaunt wolf of the desert wide
Shall 'round the carcass gnash and rave;
Some traveler, when those bones are bare,
The red feast with the vulture share.

\*      \*      \*      \*

Some leagues are flown;—far other scene
Lists to the Big Arkansas' song;
The coyote's howl tells what has been,
And white bones strew the plain along;
The red man seeks a far domain,
Nor wigwam dots the valley plain.

## THE VALLEY OF THE ARKANSAS.

Toward Mississippi's sunny shores,
She sweeps down from her mountains wild;
Her flood in broad abundance pours
Through densest forest glades beguiled.
Those waters, once the beaver's home,
The giant lizards sluggish roam.

Though mild, benignant waters sleep
Between those banks when autumn blooms,
A mad tide, raging vast and deep,
In early spring-time roaring comes;
Then woe to daring settler, should
He seek to brave that threatening flood!

The wand'ring stream through Kansas glides,
And cities gem the cheerful scene;
Man's broad plantations deck her sides,
Whose fields of verdure bask serene;
Exultingly she gleams along
And sings her ever varying song.

The Ninescach and Chisholm gleam
Through swaying boughs and flowery banks;
The plum and wild grape shade the stream,
And nod above in fruitful ranks.
Here floats wild duck with water-hen,
And marmot burrows in the fen.

Amid the valley, richly fair,
Two sister rivers, laughing, meet;
And nature yields a grateful share
Of bowery nooks, and flow'rets sweet;
And of the south-west hailed the queen,
The spires of Witchita are seen!

Reclaimed from wildest nature's home—
A wond'rous marvel of the age—
She builds the architrave and dome
Where lately echoed savage rage;
Nor lingering for lapse of years,
Wealth, beauty, fashion, art appears!

Bright gem within an emerald shrine,
The beauteous city proudly sits;
Around the grassy billows shine,
O'er which the dark green shadow flits—
Springing, as by enchantment's wand,
Her walls rise high above the land.

'Tis sweet the charming scene to view,
When browse the herds 'neath twilight skies;
As, waving 'gainst the back-ground blue,
Dark foliage to the breeze replies;

## THE VALLEY OF THE ARKANSAS.

And flowers blooming wildly fair,
Perfume the balmy evening air.

\*　　\*　　\*　　\*　　\*

Here Coronado led his horde
Of Spaniards, urged by greed of gain,
With conquest written on his sword;
The earliest pale face on this plain,
To slay its beasts and wear their fur—
The valley's bold discoverer!

A thrifty merchant Durfee was,
Who reared this Indian trading post,
When civilization gave no laws
Securing life or treasure lost;
When lawless men with crime in view
Established here their rendezvous.

But emigration's ceaseless flow
Soon overawes these sons of crime—:
And settlers' vigorous actions show
Grim retribution bides her time,
Till gallows tree by moonlight dim,
Bears horse thief swung from every limb!

The desperado's deeds no more
Restraints of civil law defy;
The day of Ledford's League is o'er,
And violence beheld him die,
Fighting foes fiercely, hand to hand,
Betrayed by one his early friend.

# LEDFORD'S LEAGUE.

# LEDFORD'S LEAGUE.

'TIS half-a-score of years ago
    Since Ledford fell before his foe—
His face is still remembered well;
And thrilling tales the settlers tell
Of his bold deeds, and plundering band,
When from the tree-top sprang the yell
Of catamount o'er twilight land;
And sullen nature held her ban
O'er savage beast and wolfish man.

He was a man of daring deed;
And smooth of tongue; in manner mild;
No soul so well prepared to lead
Marauders of the prairie wild.
But generous at times, and brave,
He interposed his stern command,
And turned aside the murd'rous hand,
And aid to needy settler gave.

A horseman formed for fleetest steed—
Unerring shot at lightning speed!
A card displayed five crimson spots—
Along the tube glanced Ledford's eye;
His weapon flashed five deadly shots—
Each bullet bore a spot away!
Such feat—a score of steps removed—
His matchless skill as marksman proved.

A black man sat astride his mule;
Sat somnolent with blinking eye—
Firm fingers clenched his yielding wool,
And Ledford's charger fleet flew by!
Held high, and howling 'bove the plain,
His dangling feet ne'er touch the ground;
Wild laughter greets his cry of pain,
From rude frontiersmen gathered 'round.

What wonder, then, he thought that day
Foul Lucifer bore him away!
The devil and Tom Walker ne'er
More swiftly sped for hades drear!—
Thus Ledford's strength and skill subdued
His band of spirits fierce and rude.

'Twas not the love of cruel act,
Nor greed that loved ill-gotten gain,
That made him outlaw of the plain;
Things such as these could ne'er attract.
The thrilling scenes of early life,
Those years with fierce adventure rife,
Hair-breadth escapes that mark the past,
Insatiate love bred in his breast
For desperate dangers of the west.

The nation's scout, he won renown;
Intrepid, brave, excelled by none.
Familiar things were wounds to him,
Who bore their scars on every limb;
And they were myriad on his breast,
As many an eye could well attest,
That knew the heart of Ledford best.

To him he chose to name a friend,
His truth was steadfast to the end;
Remorselessly he slew his foe,
And vengeance he would e'er forego.

\*　　\*　　\*　　\*　　\*　　\*

A cavern wild, to few revealed,
Dense thickets deep within the shore

The robbers' rendezvous concealed,
Who to its shades their plunder bore.
'Twas wide within, that refuge cave,
And entered from the darkened wave
Where tangled roots, and bending sedge
Drooped o'er it's densely shaded edge,
Which wove a thick umbrageous door,
Fringed high above with mosses hoar
That hung from tree trunks mottled dark,
Where basked the snake on glossy bark.

The entrance hid by foliage green,
Five hundred horse might stand within;
Secure concealed from all without,
Where silent waters spread about,
Which ne'er betrayed where hoof had been.

Far in the cavern, dark and deep,
A break gave means of swift escape;
And when was danger imminent,
A sentinel the signal sent;
Should foe perchance e'er enter there,
He might but find deserted lair.

They hied them here the foe to foil,
'Twas here they met for midnight raid;

Here gathered to divide the spoil;
Here died the traitor who betrayed.

\* \* \* \* \* \*

By shades of night obscured, away
The bold marauder urged his prey—
A splendid steed, a stolen prize—
To where his mystic pathway lies;
Eluding by his arts acute
The foemen hotly in pursuit;
Plunging in deepest shade he flies,
Engulfed in night's dark mysteries.

Now he beholds Arkansas gleam—
Swift plashes down the shallow stream;
A league pursues his watery way
To where the sheltering cavern lay.
There through dense shadows none can see
The daring bandit disappear.
He parts the wild vines now, and he
Beyond pursuit knows naught of fear.

Pursuers baffled, long in vain
Search eager for the trail again;
The shining waters hide the track,
And flash their mild defiance back.

Within the cavern comrades greet;
Praise, while they stroke the charger fleet;
Then, neath the torch's flickering glare,
The bandits spread their homely fare.
No danger near, they fain resign
Their care to quaff the cheering wine;
And many a daring, desperate deed,—
Aye, deeds of horror and of blood!
Recount they there beside that flood
Slow rippling by; nor stops to heed
The frequent oath, the ruder jest
O'er narrative of lawless quest.

A stranger 'mid the murderous band
Frivolous gamed with dextrous hand;
Swore desp'rate oaths as loud as they,
As interest deepened in the play.
A counterfeiter from the north,
Dispensed queer coins at Leavenworth;
Discovered, men were on his track—
Had thrice escaped from prison cell;
Pursuit was foiled—foes turned them back,
And he 'mid scenes remote would dwell.

Such was the tale—'twas smoothly told,
With swag'ring air and feature bold;

But something in his wavering eye
Had not been passed unheeded by.
There were dread signs that boded ill—
Signs terrible 'mong men who kill!

Dark lowering brows aside were bent;
Strange looks, and nods significant;
Low mutt'rings breathed a hated name—
A vigilanter? spy?—the same!

One on the trigger placed a hand;
Then scowled inquiringly about
With glance not hard to understand.
One rose, and cautious peered without—
A deadly flash—a fleeting ball—
A bleeding wound—a heavy fall;
And lo! Along the crimson floor,
Their guest lay groaning in his gore.

The robber chief the writhing form
Beheld, then strode to where he lay;
Looked on the life-blood gushing warm,
And heard the lips for mercy pray
Between the struggling gasps for breath,
In lingering agony of death.

"Poor fellow, I will be a friend;
Your misery this hand shall end."

The weapon gleamed from out his belt;
The shining steel the pressure felt;
The bullet found the throbbing brain,
And death was there to end his pain.

Oh, could that river murmuring low,
Tell of dark deeds she witnessed there,
Her bosom dyed in crimson glow,
From that cold shape her waters bear,
Ye'd learn low from her yellow bank
That form was flung—and sullen sank.

\*      \*      \*      \*      \*

Lone traveler through this region drear,
Deems all secure, nor harbors fear.
With weapons clenched and watchful eye,
The outlaws close beside appear,
Crouched neath that clump he passes by.
They spring before the startled team!
A short resistance bids him die!
No ear to heed his pleading cry;

The night winds moan responsive sigh—
They plunge his body in the stream.

The wild-cat rent the stilly air,
Like some lone goblin of despair;
At midnight deep, the panther's scream
Breaks on the bandit's troubled dream.

\*         \*         \*         \*         \*

A TIME the daring bandit chief
Wearied of strife, and sought relief
From every rude and dismal scene,
Where peace and quietude convene.

Though fierce in brawling border fight,
He well was skilled in arts polite;
With bearing high, of manly grace;
And smiles were frequent on his face.
And oft he came, a welcome guest,
To settler's thrifty border home;
Where fair ones' smiles full oft confest
Their hearts beat faster when he come.

And there was one his soul subdued,
Who strove to lure him from this way,

That stained his hand full oft with blood,
In deeds that shun the light of day.


The fair and gentle Alice loved,
And Ledford's fiery spirit moved
To quit for aye the desp'rate band
He long had led with dauntless hand.
He learned a lawful, peaceful art;
Resigned him to love's fond command,
And Alice reigned within his heart.


He grew a leader in the game
That pleased the hardy frontier crew;
And warm admirers round him drew,
Whose praises bore afar his fame.


Without their dauntless brave to lead
The fierce attack, the midnight raid,
The desperadoes grew dismayed,
And to their leader's voice gave heed.
They followed still their hero chief;
They learned like him the arts of peace;
The vale rejoiced at crime's decrease—
They plowed the land, they bound the sheaf.

The settlers' daughters made them wives,
Who knew to tame the heart of man;
And in their peaceful homes began
To bless with happiness their lives.

The ruder ruffian failed to find
Contentment 'neath domestic roof;
Nor from the old life held aloof—
There came to him nor peace of mind.
His restless spirit spurned restraint;
And deep and loud his oft complaint,
While he drained deep the firey bowl.
Then loud defying every law
That would their lawlessness control,
Wildly they rode through Wichita,
With weapons blazing while they sped,
And townsmen shrank, and women fled!

Full oft—and madness rules the day—
They clenched, and fought in fierce affray;
Quick oaths—red knives that gleam again—
A fall—a groan—a comrade slain!
Completing many a mad career,
Borne to the grave on blood-stained bier.

'Mong these—a man of roughest mold—
Was Marshall; second in command,
Lieutenant long of Ledford's band;
Unlike his chief in many a way;
Fierce tiger when he stood at bay;
Like him renowned for spirit bold.


Wed with a girl of low estate—
A beautiful unfortunate—
The ruffian's rudeness broke her heart;
She grew aweary of the world,
And long endured grief's bitterest smart,
Till patience from her throne was hurled.


Her own hand mixed the fatal draught;
Her lips the deadly poison quaffed;
Then, e'er those lips in death were sealed,
She to the monster's soul appealed.
With glazing eye she bade him stay
His steps so long in evil way;
Plead with weak voice, and failing breath:
"Six moons," she said, "shall pass you by,
And by my side your form shall lie."
True prophecy! 'Twas as she said—
Six moons, and Marshall, too, lay dead!

\* \* \* \* \* \*

AMID such joys as Ledford knew,
He learned to love the good, the true.
A few short weeks of wedded life—
O, happy weeks! O, happy wife!
Still one destroying trait was kept;
Down deep within his bosom slept
A hatred cruel as the grave—
One injury he ne'er forgave.
He vowed—and 'twas no idle threat,
"When I shall see the knave, he dies!
I'll shoot Jack Bridges 'twixt the eyes!"
Nor was he known to e'er forget.

Then Bridges learned of Ledford's vow,
Serving as minion of the law.
Ere long he sped to Wichita,
Alert for vengeance—Ledford's life;
And burned to meet his foe in strife.

A comrade to the valley came—
Perfecting plans—a deadly game—
For, well might Bridges fear to call
His whilome chief to deadly brawl;
Their past adventures served to tell

His foeman's prowess all too well;
And now he sought, well armed, to lay
In ambush for his wily prey.

A troop of cavalry to aid,
Lay close concealed within the shade
Of sombre grove of cotton-wood,
That by the river's margin stood.

The spies thought Ledford from the town,
And strolled, suspecting not the foe.
The way turned suddenly—when, lo!
They met his fierce, menacing frown.
The flames of malice ne'er abate,
O'er unforgotten deed of hate—
No wrath like that of former friends;
Only in death their hatred ends.

The unarmed Ledford sprang away,
Then faced his foes, and stood at bay
Behind a friendly sheltering shed,
Prepared to close in combat dread.

A friendly hand threw weapons there—
Firm clenched, they flash!—when, from his lair

The outlaw sprang as Bridges fell,
Whose comrade swift avenged his fall;
And sent the hotly spinning ball,
Aimed too unerringly and well—
To find a lodgment in his breast;
Another shot!—a shattered wrist!

The bandit over Bridges stood,
All crimsoned o'er with streaming blood;
And while the earth life's current drank,
Doomed Ledford's failing weapon sank
Impotent o'er his prostrate foe,
Scarce injured yet—though fallen low,
And similating death, he lay,
While faint his foeman turned away.

His quivering limbs could illy bear
The outlaw's form beyond the spot,
Where friendly hands bestowed their care;
But death had winged the fatal shot—
He knew the messenger was nigh;
Then, e'er he closed for aye his eye:
"Speak, have I killed him?" "No," they said;
And then—the bandit chief was dead.

WICHITA, April, 1881.

# A PRAIRIE ROMANCE.

# A PRAIRIE ROMANCE.

AMID the grandeur of the East,
    Where wealth piled high her plentitude,
A youthful pair, from care released,
In one bright, blissful dream abode,
Till youth's ambition bore away
The sun that lit the maiden's day.

Though Helen's hand to him resigned
Would more than competence insure,
Warren's nobility of mind
Forbade to wed while he was poor.
Entreaties failed; farewell's were said;
Far to the sunset land he sped.

Sweet maiden, there were none to share
Thy woes; with blooming youth had grown
That tender passion; bleak dispair

Were doubly thine, could'st thou have known
Those anxious years of hope and pain,
E'er Warren's arms should clasp again.


Oh, fairest Helen! richly blest
With loveliest attributes of mind,
Thy form of moulded grace possessed
The budding charms of womankind;
With gentlest dignity of pride,
Received from sire's aspiring tide.


There be who are, some are not wise,
So runs the world eternally,
'Mid maidens' tears and lovers' sighs,
And murmured vows of constancy;
Howbeit, months, aye! years of gloom
With disappointments' woes do come.


Oh, when through fickle fortune's frown,
Grim failure sneers at every turn,
And bows the soul in sadness down,
Oh, where shall man submission learn?
So mused the sire of Helen, when
With her he sought the spreading plain.

Far in the West a quick retrieve
Was promised for his fortune's wreck;
Where otter, wolf, and badger, give
The soft fir circling beauty's neck;
And dusky warriors in return,
Fire-arms and loved fire-water earn.

Bright naiad of Arkansas' stream!
Such soft, brown hair and hazel eyes
Oft wakens admiration's beam,
And bids the fond emotions rise—
Those eyes no soft responses dart,
For Warren lives in Helen's heart.

Still, constancy in her pure breast
Abode, amid misfortune's woes;
Hope cheered their journeyings through the West,
And forced the pensive smile that rose,
E'en while she traced the line to tell
Her wand'ring lover what befell.

\*    \*    \*    \*    \*

On, why seek fortune, name and fame,
When frowns the whole world cold and dark?

How can ambition's glowing flame
Shed through the soul its vital spark?
Thus, Warren—Helen false or dead—
On dark, dispairing fancies fed.

He languished; still no message came
To cheer him through the toiling days;
Though many missives bore her name,
He found her not. So time delays
'Mid hoping, waiting. Thus it is,
Bleak disappointments banish bliss!

The restless child of scowling fate,
Intent on drowning gloomy care,
With scarce a ling'ring hope elate,
Denounced the city's baleful glare;
Where toilsome nights beheld his pen
Portray the griefs and joys of men.

Lured by the rumors floating far,
Perfumed by prairie's breath of balm,
Seeking to prove if clouds can mar
Such scenes so fair and wildly calm.
Of sweet forgetfulness in quest,
He hied him to the famed Southwest.

# A PRAIRIE ROMANCE.

Oh, waft ye, fragrant zephyrs, from
Long bending grass and pictured hills!
From nature's gorgeous gardens come
And laugh with all your rippling rills!
Oh, spread your glowing beauties out—
I hail you with a joyous shout!

He heard the boom of prairie hen,
That roused him with the morning star;
Sought brant and wild goose 'mid the fen,
And chased the fleet jack-rabbit far;
Pursued beyond the valley' slope
The graceful bounding antelope.

The sensitive plant's rare, ruby tint,
By young winds fed with silver dew,
In settings of the fragrant mint,
Shrinks from his touch—as maidens do
Before the glance their beauty claims,
When ardent admiration flames.

No gleaming dome of palace grand,
In dazzling grandeur greets his eye,
Where unpretentious dwellings stand,
He might not view admiringly;

No span 'bove the Arkansas stood,
Where wave the silvery cottonwood.

A strangely mingled group was there,
As rude the infant hamlet lay;
Bold borderers with flowing hair,
Who wond'rous skill in chase display—
Adventurers of every grade,
With enterprising sons of trade.

That frontier's luxuries were few,
Though fashion came with polished arts;
For, beauty here had wandered, too,
To win and tame the ruder hearts;
And oftentimes a deeper shade
Tinged the brown cheek of native maid.

Oh, many a mirthful gathering there
The prairie moon smiled down upon,
As joyously the young and fair
Whirled the gay dance till night was gone—
Their sprightly pipe and viol ne'er
To sound in splendor's halls would dare.

\*      \*      \*      \*      \*

Beguiled by sportive comrades gay
One eve, where whirled the dizzy dance,
Young Warren gazed admiringly,
With more than rapture in his glance,
On one fair form of matchless grace—
Her face shone on him—Helen's face!

'Twas his heart's idol, lost—and found:
In glad surprise and wild delight
She sought his arms, that close enwound,
To tell the story of her flight;
And speak of halcion years to come,
With him in their sweet valley home.

"Dear Warren, I have mourned for you,
Not knowing where my love was flown;
Oh, how could you think her untrue
Whose faithfulness these years have shown?
Our happiness shall not be less,
Though fate has lingered long to bless.

"Far other scenes beheld us reared,
'Mong friends remote, in other time,
Before misfortune's clouds appeared,
Before I sought the western clime;

Nor dreamed, then, such secluded spot
Should e'er be mine or Warren's lot."

"Oh, Helen! could I dream or know
That I should find my darling here?
The lowering future fails to show
The blessings she so soon shall bear.
Blest be my unseen guiding star,
That lured me to my bride afar."

No moon e'er shone with milder light,
Enthroned mid skies of deeper blue,
Than softly shines this balmy night,
Suggestive of the good, the true,
As reunited, side by side,
Strays Warren and his blooming bride.

'Mid that rejoicing scene he found
One flower that cheered the valley fair,
Whose potent magic quickly drowned
The woes he illy strove to bear;
And two hearts throbbed in pure delight,
When joy sprang forth from sorrow's night.

# HANK HAWKINS,

# THE SHOWMAN.

# HANK HAWKINS, THE SHOWMAN.

SILENT signs of man's art in the midst of the plain,
    By long grass o'erhung, still the earth-pits remain,
Where nature unvanquished, dominion declares,
'Mid lifeless, deserted, and dim thoroughfares;
Converging from distant points, hither they meet,
Where the long, level prairie paths merged in a street.
Habitations of men in the distance arise,
Indenting the regular rim of the skies,
Where the wide prairie rolls to the horizon's bar,
And the fragrant wild rose spreads its odors afar;
Undisturbed by the voice of man's toil-laden dream,
Here the spirit of solitude reigneth supreme.

    The river, light-skirted by green cottonwood,
Bends away to the eastward; here Park City stood,—
But where are her dwellings that gleamed o'er the plain,
And cheered the worn emigrant's famishing train?

Fair Sedgwick, exulting! 'tis thine to reply—
Alluring her people, beholding her die.
The ringing rail gleams at thy glad trader's door,
And thy rival's existence disturbs thee no more.
Now the site of Park City is all that remains
Of the beautiful village, the pride of the plains.

Hank Hawkins, a hardy young denizen, came,
And hard by the hamlet was holding a claim;
Heroically striving through hardship and toil,
To kill the wild nature that clung to the soil;
Inverting the prairie grass never disturbed
By the might of the steed that the plowman had curbed;
Industriously strewing the ground with the grain,
While strange projects formed in his versatile brain.
Ambition's stern struggles brought ceaseless unrest,
And a longing for eminence woke in his breast;
And how to attain the desire of his heart,
Was the dream that refused from his brain to depart.

Like Nimrod of old, the first huntsman of might,
Hank Hawkins pursued the wild chase with delight;
His success as a huntsman his cabin attests,
Which the fur of wild animals thickly invests.
Here roam through the valley the buffalo brown,

Bear, badger and otter. Fur, finer than down,
A carpet for comfort and luxury made,
And a couch of soft skins in the room is displayed.
Like Little Red Ridinghood's bed, there appears
By the pillow protruding a pair of wolf's ears;
The huge claws of bruin decorating one side,
While dangling beyond hangs the badger's gray hide;
Below, mottled skins of the antelope meet,
And the couch of Hank Hawkins is soft and complete.


Near the door of the domicile, held by a chain,
A bear cub reposes at length on the plain;
Occasionally growling complaints at his foes,
The mischievous insects that tickled his nose;
A cowardly coyote concluding his meal,
Behind the rude kennel his form would conceal;
Two brown, cunning prairie dogs gambol before
The opening that serves for the cabin's rude door;
A beautiful antelope sports in high glee,
Like a bird lightly bounding, as graceful and free;
A black wolf is snarling and gnawing a bone;
A buffalo calf stands impatient, alone,
And sullenly stamping diminutive hoof,
From a natural enemy holding aloof.

The lord of the motley assemblage, perusing
A train of deep thought, o'er the picture is musing.
His lank figure leans by an earth-planted beam,
While his bronze features bend to the play of his
    dream—
Then Hawkins deliberately strode from his place,
With his chin in his palm, stern resolve in his face;
Complaisantly raised the broad brim from his brow,
And breathed in these words a significant vow:
"I'll do it, for what is the good stayin' here?—
So soon as I've gathered my melons this year,
My menagerie shall move: for I must see the sights—
Won't I take in the money, those days and those nights?
Thare's Hammond won't mind lookin' after the claim
Till I can come back agin, bringin' a name.
Indianaians never saw varmints like them—
I warrant they'd shy from that lazy bar, Jim!

"I calculate it's a considerable plan
To hunt all these animals up, and a man
Deserves suthin' more than jist 'thanky,' to drive
Cl'ar back to the States with the critters alive!
They ought to be glad to come into my show,
For nateral hist'ry is suthin' to know.
I'll start in the show business sartin' and sure,
And it's time I was travellin' round on my tour.

There's no reason on 'arth why I can't afford
To fetch up a Barnum, or Artemus Ward!—
Thunderashun! how awful them Hoosiers'll laugh,
To gaze at the pranks of this buffaler calf!"

Hank roused up the bear from his nap in the sun;
The villainous wolf, having finished his bone,
Round his well trodden range began restlessly pacing,
As the keeper his steps to the hut was retracing.
As he stood by the cabin, long time did he pore
O'er the lumber that lay by his domicile door,
Perfecting his plans.

"I'll jest fix up them cages
A slashin' round swifter'n if workin' fur wages.
The varmints all orter have bars to their dens—
'Twon't seem much like standin' out here on the plains.
I'll gear the team now, and drive down to the Park,
An' be back with the fixin's I need afore dark."

As he sped o'er the smooth, level prairie, grand
  schemes
Progressed toward completion in wonderful dreams;
Some time e'er the end of his journey was made,
His plans of procedure in detail were laid.

A route deemed propitious was planned through a region
Where the western menagerie's patrons were legion.

The Park City people praised highly the plan;
Admiringly gazed on the wonderful man!
His dens all completed, the beasts were confined,
The beautiful antelope tethered behind.
All plans are perfected, provisions secure,
Bright hope is before him, and smiles to allure.
Kind friends wish him well at the moment of starting,
And Hawkins for unexplored fields is departing.

Weary days rolled away e'er he made his first stand,
Having safely arrived in the civilized land.
All arrangements complete, he an orchestra sought—
Without music, exhibiting comes to but naught.

Disturbed were Hank's slumbers that night, and he dreamed
He possessed a huge canvas, and myriads teemed
Within and without; the full treasury groaned
With the money collected; immense wealth he owned—
The brass band discoursed a most beautiful strain,
While the lion was roaring and shaking his mane.

The lady performer, ascending the wire,
O'er the glistening top-canvas ascended still higher,
Gracefully girating in spangles and gauze,
Defiant of all gravitation's fixed laws.
Multitudes with fixed faces all heavenward gazed;
Wealth, beauty and fashion, all brilliantly blazed!
He, the richly dressed manager, chain of gold wore,
And valuable diamonds his finger-rings bore.

The music clashed loudly, and thousands pressed in;—
Then a thunder-storm broke with a deafening din,
And the wind pulled the stakes, and the center-poles fell;
Loud roared the wild beasts; with a terrible yell!
The lightnings flashed fiercely! the people complained;
The wagon was struck that the treasure contained!
With the anguish he woke,—and what ended his pain
Was his own bear uneasily rattling his chain!

Next morn as he strode through the midst of his
    beasts,
Grown thinner through travel—when few were their
    feasts—
Consuming solicitude surged in his breast,
That dream having left him careworn and oppressed.
Then the band of musicians in promptitude came,

With the radiant rising of day's cheerful flame;
And their lively strains floated from trumpet and drum,
Commingling e'er long with the crowd's happy hum.
Multitudes through the entrance in fitful streams pour,
To the keeper transferring admission fees o'er,
Whose features ne'er glistened so brightly before.

The rustic amazement was quaintly expressed,
As they gazed at the "varmints" from far away West.
How they laugh at the moods of the sullen young bison;
Their cudgels the black wolf sets teeth like a vice on;
The antelope's mottles fair fingers caress,
And the teeth of the coyote are gnashed in distress;
While the showman is frequently forced to repair
Where the *gamin* too roughly are teasing the bear.
At shadows of night-fall the people disperse,
And Hawkins complaisantly makes up his purse.

'Twas varying success as again and again
The menagerie was shown from the far away plain—
Then the skies frowned upon him with terrible rain.
He had sought a fair village, yet people came not,
The torrents preventing their reaching the spot.

How vainly he waited, as day after day
Came landlord and butcher demanding their pay,

For the last of his treasure had vanished away.
While the floods were descending, he soliloquised:
"Hank Hawkins, you needn't be any surprised
If yer luck's goin' back on yer—I r'aly vow
An elephant's trod on this pocket-book, now!
My varmints an' me had jest better pull out;
If we can't have fair weather, we'll travel without."

Another location e'er long he had found—
A village of Hoosiers distributed round
On claybanks and gullies. Convenient room
Was procured in the midst of misgiving and gloom.
A town without music!—unkempt and uncouth
Are the denizens of such a hamlet, forsooth!

Through the ominous quietude scarcely a score
Apathetically sought the menagerie's door.
The "Van Winkles" cared not for the wonderful West,
Twenty leagues from their homes they had never progressed.
E'en the few who the price of admission would spare,
Knew naught of the land of the bison and bear,
And the other queer quadrupeds there to be shown,
Supposing they probably fell from the moon.

Ill fortune continued; vast volumes of rain
Continued to deluge the hill and the plain.
Solitary, solicitous, lone in the gloom,
Hank waited the measure of merciless doom.
Growled the animals grim o'er their scanty repast,
As the bailiff approached with a warrant at last;
Harshly threatening with seizure menagerie *en masse*,
Exhibiting which he declared a trespass
On the laws of the town, unless license were paid,
Which Hawkins, per force without funds, had delayed—
Nor the sum so desirable could he produce;
He ruefully muttered, "The devil's let loose!"

The bailiff unscrupulous seized the possessions,
Unloosing the chains with the harshest expressions.
The brutes in their struggles were terribly rude,
Till the officer's cudgel their tempers subdued.
Then their keeper's blood boiled as he powerless gazed,
Dispairing, heart-broken, stupefied and amazed.

Alas, 'twas the drama enacted again,
That causes mankind at the fates to complain.
Can it be, only heart-desolation is born
Of the hopes that rise joyous as lark in the morn?
Hank Hawkins returned to his home on the plains,
Hard by where the site of Park City remains.

# THE PRAIRIE FIRE.

# THE PRAIRIE FIRE.

WINDING southward, flow two rivers with a valley
    fair between,
On whose banks in Autumn twilight clam'rous water-
    fowl convene;
And their myriads repassing have abundant gleanings
    found,
Where the settler reapt a harvest from the generous
    yielding ground.
Many a homestead rides the billow of the brown plain
    rolling wide;
Humble herald of the palace brought by civilization's
    tide.

Sturdy youth led giant oxen daily to the fragrant hay,
Reared like castles heavenward pointing, landmarks o'er
    the lonely way;
Round the isolated homestead by the wild Arkansas'
    shore,

Where the matron held dominion and the frontier's hardship's bore.

Oh, ye dwellers in great cities, with luxurious comforts blest,
Wot ye of heroic woman who undaunted tames the West?
Who from fortune's wrecks have gathered what the whirlwind scattered far,
When misfortunes culminating mingled in commercial war?

\* \* \* \* \*

Late in Autumn youth and matron looked upon the lurid sky;
'Mid the ranks of tall grass bending, by the grain-fields rustling nigh;
Heard the clamours of the wildfowl, numerous sweeping overhead;
Heard the grinding from the manger, where the beasts of burden fed;
And the shrill-voiced swine complaining, and the cackl'ing neath the shed.

Tempered by the fragrant breezes, summer's balmy breath had past;

## THE PRAIRIE FIRE.

Now the prairie's pictured gardens bend before the biting blast.
From Sierra's snow-clad summit sweeps the spinning simoon down,
O'er the homestead's fertile acres with their verdure painted brown.

Round their cot the prairie ocean—by their plainly-spread repast,
Plans projecting for the morrow—sudden o'er the valley cast,
'Gainst the smoth'ring, sullen heavens spreads a winding sable scroll,
'Midst a roar like surges crashing, or the mut'ring thunder's roll.

Smitten with wild consternation leapt the youth beyond the door—
Flashed broad sheets of flame before him—nearer, louder grew the roar!
Through the grass-roots firey serpents writhing 'neath dense vapors gleam!
High athwart the hot horizon, blood-streaked pyramids of flame
Dance along the Big Arkansas, eastward o'er her sister stream!

Conflagrations sweep the dwellings from the smoke-
　　beclouded lands;
Leaping hedgerows, roads and rivers—naught the fear-
　　ful flame withstands.
Swiftly sweeps the demon phalanx, like the dreadful day
　　of doom,
And the hot breath, all devouring, welcomes to a firey
　　tomb.


On and onward, redly rolling, lashed to frenzy by the
　　blast,
Terror-stricken herds pursuing, sweep destruction's
　　surges fast.
See! the flames sweep through the grain-fields—round
　　them plays the lurid light!
While the youth and matron nerve them for the hot, un-
　　equal fight.


But the lone cot stood protected by the bald clay beat-
　　en round,
And the flames defeated stayed them, neither leapt the
　　barren ground,
And the home stood an oasis by the flaming desert
　　bound.

## THE PRAIRIE FIRE. 55

Cries of horror from the mother drew the son's gaze
    from his toil,
As the fire-fiend's jaws insatiate seize the granaries for
    his spoil!
Long they lash the frantic fire, striving wearily in vain—
Shrieks from shrill-voiced swine proceeding—fowls are
    flut'ring o'er the plain;
In wild neighings from the stable tells the frantic horse
    his fright,
While the bellowing cattle breaking from their tethers
    speed their flight.

Sprang the youth to free the horses, where the glowing
    furnace stood,
Heeding not the choking vapors or the glowing cotton-
    wood;
Quick the mad steed liberated, sped before the fiery
    train—
Terror lends its wings—escaping 'mong the creatures of
    the plain;
But the wild flames leaping after in a hot pursuit for
    prey,
To the mustang were familiar, that before them darts
    away!
Still the youth who rescued, lingers 'mong the rafters
    falling round;

Scorching flames roar through the entrance where he
  needs must pass beyond,
And the smoke that wraps is smoth'ring; and the flames
  are in his eyes—
Sinks upon the glowing threshold—blist'ring, blinded.—
  Grief, surprise
Smite the mother as she drags him from the hot embrac-
  ing flame—
O'er the seared and lifeless body wrought till animation
  came.

 \* \* \* \* \*

 Darkly beautiful at evening when the flames have hur-
  ried by,
Are the lurid night-fires gleaming 'gainst the redly-tint-
  ed sky!
When the satiate foe retiring from his desolated track,
Halts at intervals, and camp-fires flash fantastic menace
  back!

 Far around beyond the rivers, the horizon's golden
  rim
Glows anon with gleaming grandeur!—soon is veiled in
  twilight dim.
Like the flight of brilliant genius, startling for a time
  the world—

Wanes the meteors—swiftly fading, down oblivion's waters hurled.

\* \* \* \* \* \*

From the hamlet far returning, late the weary settler came
To his homestead desolated by the devastating flame,
To behold his lonely dwelling looming o'er the blackened wild!
Scarce a vestige of his garners—save a heap of ruins piled.
Still his spirit is undaunted, though his winter stores are burned,
Still his broad lands spread around him—smiling fields are soon returned.

Neighboring settlers' wives and children, homeless, shiv'ring in the blast,
Hover round their smould'ring ruins mid the desolation vast;
Nor a vestige e'en remaining, save what clings about the form
Of the store of raiment gathered, 'gainst the biting winter storm.

Yes, 'tis well, man still redeemeth human nature from its wrong,

By warm charities dispensing the unfortunate among—
Products of long years of labor swept away—restored
 again;
The frontiersman, persevering, builds his city on the
 plain.

# THE CARNIVAL

# OF DEATH.

*This poem, with the shorter ones that immediately follow, the scene of which was Newton, record but the facts; as the settlers of that now flourishing city can testify.*

# THE CARNIVAL OF DEATH.

## PART I.

### NEWTON.—THE TEXANS.

COME, hardy pioneers who dared
    To brave the western wild,
And these broad prairies early shared
    With nature's swarthy child,
And hear this faithful history
Of Newton, by the Santa Fe.

Wild nature's prairies, broad and fair,
    Unbroken by the steel,
Rich as Euphrates' valleys were,
    Their treasures would reveal
To hearts heroic here to come,
Possess the land, and rear a home.

The railroad pierced the prairies green;—
  Topeka saw begun
The gleaming line to lay between
  The Mexic mountains dun:
Vast riches to convey afar
From where the hoof-trod *llanos* are.

The shrieking engine swift conveys
  Vast multitudes who spread
Far west and south, through length'ning ways,
  Plodding with ceaseless tread;
Their couch but nature's green, until
They rear their rustic domicile.

The sturdy smith smote clanging bar,
  The craftsman rattled loud,
Broad cities rose, and gleaming far
  Stands many a village proud,
Where huge-horned oxen haul their load
From thrifty squatter's thatched abode.

\*　　\*　　\*　　\*　　\*　　\*

NEWTON was born amid the storms
  Of conflicts' fiercest blows;
Night's midnight hush heard wild alarms,
  Where friends were turned to foes,

Whose desp'rate deeds of blood forbid
From daylight's searching sun were hid.

Ah! 'twas a sanguinary place,
   Where roughs their revels kept;
Whose outcast crew—a daring race,
   While good men sweetly slept,—
Broke midnight's silent solitude
With orgies riotous and rude!

Her blood-stained cemetery proclaims
   Of darkly dreadful deeds;
Rude head-boards oft record their names
   On whom the coyote feeds,
Who fell beneath the crimson hand,
Before the law redeemed the land.

Here Texas sent her myriad herds,
   With daring drovers, wild,
And reckless as the world affords;—
   In frequent fray embroiled;
A hardy horde in wildness reared,
Whose gold was sought, whose passions feared.

To spur the steed in hottest race,
   When stampede larums the herd;

To throw the lasso in the chase,
   While *llanos* broad are scoured,
Fulfill the sum of arts pursued
   By Texan herder, fierce and rude.

He knows no law, obeys no creed,
   And where the clime that can
Produce such race for daring deed—
   Whose spirit spurns the ban
Of civilization,—whose true reign
Is o'er the herd, the steed, the plain?

But chivalrous he is, and true,
   When on his native plain,
Would his last morsel share with you,
   ' Till wine has fired his brain;
Then hot blood's brawling oaths are heard,
His friend is slain at slightest word!

\*     \*     \*     \*     \*

ALONG the trail, with trampling hoof,
   And whoop and yell they came;
Shrewd Newton vouchsafes no reproof—
   She claims the gilded game—

For, e'er he quits her streets again,
Nor coins in Texan's purse remain.


His jingling spurs with ceaseless clang,
  The pave beneath him pelt;
Two murd'rous pistols ever hang
  Suspended from his belt.
The play holds o'er him close control,—
In game of chance would stake his soul!


They stroll the streets a roist'rous route,
  Aflush with liquid flame;—
I wot, their wild, defiant shout
  Proclaims no spirit tame,
As each upon his charger leaps,
And through the town like whirlwind sweeps!


Nor fleeter may the mustang speed
  Athwart the grassy main,
Than rides this reckless renegade,
  That laws would bind in vain,
Through Newton's streets with yell and whoop,
With wild, demoniacal troop!

## PART II.

### THE AVENGER.

M ID Mexic' scenes where Rio Grande
   Her shining bound'ry rolls,
Where horn and hoof possess the land
   The ranchman's wealth controls,
There dwelt, where wide the waters flow,
The daughter of the ranchero.

Perfection's round symetric form
   Norita fair possessed;
Her moulded beauty's magic charm
   Health's fairest glow caressed,
Whose warm life current's richer glow
Was from old Spain and Mexico.

Impulsive, ardent when she loves,
   Her hatred burns the same;—
Black eyes burn fierce, when anger moves—

Beware their deadly flame!
Maid of her clime knows nought of fear,
And holds a lover's life—how dear?


Should her loved idol fall before
   Some furious foeman's hand,
Vengeance is swift—her soul's at war—
   See Mexic's maiden stand!—
Swift flash the dagger's deadly blows!
That small white hand deals death to foes!


Friend of her youth, Norita long
   Heard Riley's fervent vow;
Since childhood's day they strayed among
   These scenes; and she, e'en now,
Would list ofttimes with downcast eyes,
Yet held him hopeless of the prize.


His sweet guitar's soft serenade
   Norita near him drew;
All tender tones to charm the maid
   His skilfull fingers knew;
With him she sought—true Spanish girl—
The wild fandango's mazy whirl.

But hers was as a sister's love,
    Or light as friend of youth;
Nor knew the tender spell to move
    To life's enduring truth;
Yet 't was the light of Riley's heart,
But born to bring life's bitterest smart.

Her hand had saved his life,—one morn,
    Enraged, the lord of herds
Tossed him on high with goreing horn—
    She heard his calling words;—
With lasso thrown, securely tied,
She forced the maddened brute aside.

A life's devotion, Riley vowed;
    His steadfast soul ne'er turned;
To its fond idol mutely bowed,
    While fires consuming burned;
Sworn to repay—with life he would—
That kindly deed of hardihood.

Clusky the trader came to woo
    The black-eyed Mexic maid;
He won her heart; his vows were true;
    Soon with his bride he strayed

## THE CARNIVAL OF DEATH.

With giant herds to Newton's mart,
Well skilled in thrifty trader's art.

\*   \*   \*   \*   \*

Now Newton's day of turmoil came;
   Her people must decide
To lay the steel, or loose their fame,
   And view the iron glide
To Wichita, that burned to grasp
The ringing rail with vig'rous clasp.

The day ope'd stormy with debate;
   Contention ruled the hour;
And Bailey bore the badge of state—
   Bold herdsman—proud of power
To quell the gath'ring riot, when
Madness should rule the minds of men.

Wine flows in torrents—many a blow
   By sturdy brawler dealt,
Lays clam'rous opponent full low
   By argument he felt;
When twilight gloomed the brawling scene,
Men maudlin moved with murd'rous mien.

Bailey might not resist the bowl;—
    That eve 't was deeply drained;
Its demon gained complete control;
    His mission was disdained
By murd'rous rage—the guardian made
To force the law—nor law obeyed!

Quick Clusky came, and strove for peace,—
    Hot words in anger rose;
But while he bade the turmult cease,
    Swift through the thronging foes
Flashed Bailey's weapon!—by his breast
The whistling lead flew harmless past.

His Texan foe well Clusky knew
    Stood thirsting for his life;
Quick as the ball that by him flew,
    Prepared for deadly strife—
Fierce flashed his splendid weapons round,
And Bailey's life-blood stained the ground.

The treach'rous Texans of the plain,
    Amid their revels swore
They'd never seek the trail again
    Till Clusky breathed no more—

Exultant o'er their plot they grew—
"Vengeance!—his hand a comrade slew!"

The snare is set, the hour is near,
   In secret all have vowed,
Before the midnight moon appear,
   Clusky shall wear his shroud!—
By vengeful violence shall die
Where dancers meet, when mirth is high!

The fearless trader laughed at those
   Who, warning, sought to save;
In daring hardihood he chose
   The servile foe to brave—
Intimidated—he afraid?
Not though ten thousand plots were laid!

\*    \*    \*    \*    \*    \*

Music and mirth are mingling in
   The hall, where lamps are bright;
And feet trip lightly mid the din
   Where revel rules the night;—
Bright beauty beams with laughing eye,
Her charms adorned in rivalry.

The music ceased—at Clusky's side
    His pensive bride reclines:
She little dreams what ills betide
    Where wine with pleasure shines;
How brilliant ball-room's robes of snow
With life-blood's ruddy stains shall glow!

The trader's gaze on that glad throng
    Rests in abstracted mood;
He heeds them not who whirl along
    And on his dreams intrude;
E'en now, mid gaiety and life,
Thought teems with speculation rife.

With sudden start on her he gazed,
    Whose small hand pressed his arm;
Whose full dark eyes expressive raised,
    Were beaming full and warm;
Long lashes drooping dark enhance
The power of softest pleading glance.—

"Come, let us from this place away;
    Nought is there here can fill
My heart with cheerfulness—why stay
    With these forebodings ill?

Say, shall we go? Oh, well I know
You'll not deny me—may we go?"

"Norita, stay—I fain would learn
   Whom yon sombrero wears;
Him I have met;—I must discern
   If there be cause for fears;—
If 'tis his face, should that be he,
Prepare for basest treachery.

"A time in Arizona's mine,
   By thronging foes beset,
I saw a friendly dagger shine,
   With life-blood dripping wet,
Which vanished with returning peace,
But not till I saw Riley's face!

"My chiefest foe is here to-night,
   Whom I rejoiced as slain
By Riley's hand, in that fierce fight,
   Among the miner train.—
Wait but for briefest moment here
Till this gay throng the way shall clear."

\*     \*     \*     \*     \*

Two eyes that glow like living coals,
   Dart deadly gleams of hate,

As though the throng that visage scowls
   Above them while they wait—
Clusky beholds, and nerves for strife,
For now he knows 'tis life for life.


" Carrambo, Clusky! Riley's care
   Finished your foe, you thought;
The tables turned;—fair fortune here
   This fit occasion brought—
Vengeance is mine!—your forfeit soul
Flits e'er you full moon higher roll!"


The ruffian's sneering accents fall
   Harsh grating, hoarse and low;
Bold threats brave Clusky ne'er appall—
   His weapons front his foe—
" Assassin, you should know me well!
That boast your own fate shall impel!


" Beware! red-handed Anderson!
   A fitting instrument
The Texans found—Have you begun
   With murderous intent?
You prate of death!—draw first and fire!—
Receive my lead for all your ire!"

A harmless flash! The shrieking girl
  Clings close to Clusky's form;
Holds vice-like while his foe would hirl
  Away each circling arm.—
Through Clusky's neck the bullet sped;
The foe received his answering lead.

The fair avenger's jeweled hand
  Her gleaming dagger drew
To late that dear life to defend—
  Norita's steel was true,—
Deep buried in the murd'rer's side,
Who breathed one heavy sigh and died.

Reigned wild confusion—strife begun,
  A vengeful tigress she—
The fair, the daring, desperate one
  Deals terror while they flee!
With weapons swiftly aimed, and true,
Forbearance she is stranger to.

Norita's frenzy fierce defies
  The Texan foemen all;
Above her loved one's form that lies
  Low in the fatal hall;

While echoed her defiant wail,
A stranger entered from the trail!

He strode across the threshold red,
    With weapons fiercely clenched;
His dark eye gleams on Clusky dead,
    In gory garments drenched—
Two weapons flashed their deadly breath!
Two herdsmen sank and writhed in death!

And Texan after Texan falls
    Neath Riley's fearful aim.—
Fierce flies his shower of deadly balls,
    In terror's gory game.
Still the destroyer's gleaming eye
Demands its victims—see them die!

Oh! horrid view! confusion reigns,
    As from the casement springs
The stricken wretch, who trembling gains
    This haven.—Sharply rings
Those ruthless weapons!—wounded, dying,
Twelve gory forms all starkly lying!

Norita's gaze met Riley's eyes,
    And starting in that look,

O'er coming frenzied grief, surprise,
  Her frame convulsive shook—
In deed, in danger had they met,
Nor might she e'er that vow forget.

"Whence come you at this hideous hour?"
  Her quiv'ring accents broke?
He is avenged—your murd'rous shower
  Of bullets madly spoke!
But, oh! too late, alas! to save—
Who shall compose him for the grave?"

"I must!—my vow avenged his death—
  Shall save your precious life;
I will defend with latest breath—
  Quick!—flee this hideous strife!
Come, fly with me this scene of blood!
Already we too long have stood."

She threw her form upon her dead,
  But placidly and pale
That face reposed;—she raised his head;
  Her fond caresses fail
To wake from those still lips a sound,
Though arms of love he clasped around.

She shed no tear o'er love avenged—
  Long looked and sighed—"Away!"
\*    \*    \*    \*    \*    \*
Death's gory feast was well arranged
  E'er dawned the morning grey!—
Hard by, in Newton's graveyard drear,
The Texan's grassy graves appear.

Ha! 't was a blood-stained funeral,
  The drooping herdsmen made,
As bending o'er the crimson pall,
  Dark-visaged mourners laid
Each lifeless comrade neath the sod,
Who nevermore the *llanos* trod.

# LORA.

## LORA.

A BLISSFUL time was Lora's life,
    Where vernal beauties bloom;
Secluded far from civic strife,
    In peaceful prairie home;
Where blushing with the tinted flower
Her carol lightly cheered the hour.

A ghoul strayed o'er the prairie far
    In chase with hound and gun;
He saw the wild flower blooming there,
    Where easily was won
With blandishments and artful wile
The trustful heart that knew no guile.

Her wealth of love on him bestowed,
    Who knew well how to please,
Sweet Lora's soul with rapture glowed
    Pure as the balmy breeze—

Enchanted day! oh, hallowed time!
Dispeled delusion!—woe and crime!

The sympathetic tear shall start,
   Wrung by the touching tale
Warm from the crushed and bleeding heart
   Of lovely Lora pale;
Whose joys were as the glassy stream,
Till currents dark destroy its gleam.

He told of dear delights of home,
   Beguiled that truthful trust—
Oh! could dishonor to her come,
   And man betray the best,
And leave love in its agony,
That would have perished e'en for thee?

Alas! like nightshade's deadly blight
   Enwrapped in pleasing guise,
The poison lay, e'er yet the night
   Obscured the brightest skies:—
The charmer's gauzy web was flung
In plighted vow and honied tongue.

Unhappy one! 't were vain to tell
   What lured thee from thy nest;—

A lie, a promise, and thou fell—
   Believing thou wert blest.
Oblivion's mantle soon shall fall
O'er woes that tenderest hopes appal.


Life's hope is gone, that peaceful cot,
   And rapturous kiss of love;
Sweet girl, thine unexpected lot—
   A scene where horror wove
Her pall of anguish round thine heart,
So foully wronged—thy woes are short.


Grief gnawed the crushed and bleeding heart,
   Deserted in its pain;
The worm wrought ceasely to part
   Cords ne'er to knit again;
Full soon, the spirit stands at bay,
And nature bids her child away.


How small and white the lilly hand
   The deadly dagger turned
Toward that pure bosom, where the brand
   Of lewdness never burned?
Now all the light of life is flown;
Dispair the crowning deed has done.

## SONGS OF THE SOUTHWEST.

Bright gleams the steel, descends the knife,
    Athirst for crimson drink;
Warmed in that fair young bosom's life,
    Poised on death's mystic brink—
They laid her on the blood-stained bier,
Cold hearts and only strangers near.

He came again e'er Lora died;—
    Swift retribution then
Brought the destroyer to her side
    To fix her barb within
The craven soul of him who stole
Her young life's happiness—her all.

The spirit trembles on the verge
    Of time, so nearly flown;
As from death's shades the soul to urge,
    Those orbs turn to his own—
'Tis ended—and the look she gave
Haunts the destroyer to his grave.

Oh! pure as evening's silver dew!
    So pale, so innocent;
Health gave her rarest rosy hue,
    E'er thy young heart was rent;

For thou wert formed for nature's bower,
Sweet Lora, crushed and perished flower.

The lark will caroll o'er thy tomb,
   The midnight wind shall moan;
The fragrant wild rose here shall bloom,
   So beautiful and lone—
Where art thou gone? oh, spirit fair?
For only dust reposeth there!

Where shines the pale moon calmly on,
   When night obscures the plain,
They laid the form of Lora down
   Beneath the grassy main;
Where willows weep neath Luna's rays,
Where coyote roams and marmot plays.

# FRAGMENTS FROM

# NEWTON.

# THE COACHMAN OF THE MOUNTAINS.

AL SHATTUC drove the Denver stage
    Along the mountain steep;
Like lightning by the chasm's edge,
    Ten thousand fathom deep;
While whistling whip he fearless played,
And urged his leaders undismayed.

The ambushed savage strove to hold
    His passengers a prey,
But Shattuc kept, with spirit bold,
    The wiley foe at bay;
And sped unscathed and fearless through,
Through dangers crowded on his view!

He stood a hero 'mong the clan
    Of daring, hardy souls;

Excelled them all in skill—a man
   A generous heart controlls;
Ambitious that each hardy steed
Should all things fast in fleetness lead.

Wild Colorado's mountain step
   Loud echoed neath the tread
Of flying steeds that swiftly swep
   Like torrent o'er its bed
Of gleaming cliffs and channeled rocks
Whose voice the crashing thunder mocks!

The perils of the mountain road
   Are all in safety past;
The skulking savage's abode
   Has sunk from sight at last;
For Al. has found an easy drive
Where prairie hamlets rise and thrive.

From Newton to young Wichita,
   Through Sedgwick fair he sped;
They praised his greys who wondering saw
   His high vehicle red,
That o'er the prairie winding glides
While travelers peer from latticed sides.

## THE COACHMAN OF THE MOUNTAINS.

Al. Shattuc mounted as of yore,
    Behind six prancing steeds,
Strikes toward his leader far before,
    That little urging needs,—
A spring!—o'erturned!—Al's mid the crash!
Dragged neath those hoofs that madly dash!

Crushed neath his stage's ponderous wheels,
    A writhing mass he lay;
Death o'er those palid features steals—
    He perished with the day:—
"By Mary's grave there let me lie."
He said, and closed his eyes to die.

True hero! in thy calling brave!
    Oh! daring, early dead!
A tribute lies upon thy grave
    From one who with thee sped,
Through labyrinths of wilderness,
Whose verse thy prowess would confess.

# MARSHAL KING.

### THE DANCE HOUSE.

WHERE yonder light with ruddy glow
   Shoots its seductive ray,
The dance-house stands with gable low,
   And glaring frontal gay;
And stirring strains of music float
From viol's chord and bugle throat.

Here frailty holds high carnival;—
   Unenviable fame!
And deeds that purity appall
   Do cling about her name,
Whose light admirers, warmly gay
Ribaldry's flagrant jests essay.

There may be seen seductive mien;—
  From haunts of pleasure near,
Voluptuaries fair convene
  And smile as they appear;
Till revelers attendant there,
Charmed by the nymphs, led captive are.

The lamps glow brightly over all,
  And stirring music swells;
The mazy dance whirls through the hall,
  And loud-voiced mirth impells;
And clasped I wot full amorously
Are zones of sculptured symmetry.

The wild voluptuous dance proceeds,
  The wild'ring wine is poured,
And each his flushed companion leads
  Beside the banquet board;
Where passions dread assume their reign;
While madness rules the burning brain.

The ready daggers gleam below
  The broad belts of the crew;
Fair woman oft is decked, I trow,
  With murd'rous weapons, too!

Ah, me! when erring beauty strays,
What power shall curb, what guide her ways?

\*     \*     \*     \*     \*     \*

About the hall the lamps were bright;
   And painted beauty shed
Its artificial charm that night,
   When riot raised its head!
King came when rose wine's wild alarms;
Demanding men resign their arms!

Defiant Edwards fiercely drew
   The weapon at his belt;
His eye along the barrel threw,
   And death's dread pangs were felt,
By daring King who strove for law,
Whose thronging friends fleet vengeance vow.

It well behooved the slayer, then,
   To mount in hottest haste,—
Ride fleetly forth with might and main,
   By eager hundreds chased;
And swift as speeds the prairie gale,
He shot like arrow o'er the trail!

What charger might o'ertake him there?
　　Fool's folly 'twere to come!
As well pursue the viewless air,
　　As Edwards toward that home
Which he in safety fleetly found
Unscathed, to roam on Texan ground!

Poor King! too well your mournful end
　　Is through the region known;
Sure retribution shall attend,
　　With fury's fiercest frown,
The hand that slew where duty called,
The trust that danger ne'er appalled.

# RUIN!

"MERCHANT'S EXCHANGE," the building bore
   In lettering broad and plain;
The mien its dark frequenters wore,
   Proclaimed them men who deign
To sink a name, risk life, and swim
Through seas of blood in calling grim.

Bill Dow knew how to lay the plot
   That 'lured the Texan in,
And few might enter there and not
   Observe his wager win;
Save when for mere delusion, he
Lost through his own chicanery.

The trustful rustic left his claim
   With heavy laden van;
Returned with neither cash nor team,
   A poorer, wiser man;

For he had left his hard-earned cash
Where Newton's spiders wove their mesh.

Ambitious Dow his victim drew
  By band of music, placed
Upon pretentious stage in view
  Of passers by, who gazed
Upon the fair display within,
Nor probed the schemer's device thin.

When once he entered there—alack!
  A lamb well shorn he was
By that rough gang, who sent him back
  A mourner with good cause—
In poverty to curse the scheme,
That thus beguiled him of his team.

The keeper of the den was known
  Well through the broad Southwest;
The herdsmen of the trail had grown
  Familiar with the pest;
For minions who had little reck
Of consequence came at his beck.

You might perceive from morn till eve,
  The Texan herder ride;

# RUIN.

Hard by, secured with lasso, leave
   His steed, his wealth and pride,
To deal in game for which he burned,
Well picked, perchance, e'er he returned.

\*    \*    \*    \*    \*    \*

The Gold Room—noted gambling den—
   Doc. Thayer long had kept;
About him gathered desp'rate men,
   Whose vigilance ne'er slept,
But diligently plied their trade—
A fortune lost—as quickly made.

Doc. Thayer was a compound strange
   Of what was bad and good;
Remorseful pangs unbid would range,
   And on his soul intrude;
Though good thoughts flew with fleetest wings,
Doc. reverenced religious things!

He brought the preacher, who was heard
   Amid the jingling gold;
Beyond the bar was preached the "word,"
   With precepts good and old;

When the collection hat went round,
Rich recompense was ready found.

Where glittering games of chance were spread,
    Mock-auction, monte, keno,
And each its willing victims bled
    Round mystic tables green—Oh!
How well hoodwinked was rustic eye,
Weak plaything of grim destiny.

# THE SCORGE OF LOCUSTS.

THE settler, wearied with his toils,
    Exulting scanned his fair domain;
Dreamed of vast harvests, when rich spoils
Of giant fruits and golden grain
Should pile his garner's plenteous stores
When Boreas through the valley roars;

    Dreamed o'er improvements for the land,
Late wrested from wild nature's hold;
Of new enclosures;—fancy planned
A domicile that should enfold
His babes with greater comfort; then
His eye fell on the fields again.

    Like Egypt's devastating cloud,
Came down the locusts—hungry host!
That morn, green waved plantations broad,

That eve their verdure all was lost!
Wherever vegetation grew
The hope destroying myriads flew!

Their flights eclipse the sun with grey,
Their myriad legions ride the gale;
The scorge descends, and still they stay
Till hunger desolates the vale;
Grim Famine's ghastly face appears,
With infant moans and woman's tears.

But man has grown humane to man,
And from his plenteous garners piled,
The philanthropic current ran
With plenty for the settler's child;
And the succeeding year restored
Ten fold what fed that insect horde!

# DAWNING DAY.

THROUGH red'ning clouds that westward roll,
    The dawning daylight peers,
To cheer the steadfast settler's soul,
    Proclaiming peaceful years;
His children throng the busy halls,
Where learning's voice to wisdom calls.

The hamlet long the lawless home
    Of mad, marauding men,
Allures the tradesman; craftsmen come
    And all the arts begin,
With industries of lawful trade—
Eject the wilhom race dismayed.

Young men and maidens, and a bride
    Trod Newton's crimson ground;
Bennett had for his sweetheart sighed;

Far journeying east, he found
Devoted love prepared to come
And make these ruder scenes her home.

How brilliant were the lamps that night
   In Bentley's mansion, where
Amid a scene of mirth and light
   Was Bennett's bride, so fair?
There, from rude cabins, many a dame
To greet the bridal party came.

Now peaceful Newton calmly sits,
   Nor recks of shriek and blood,
That larmed her night; for, oh! she quits
   Her sanguinary mood;
And her broad prairies, rolling far,
Gemmed o'er with many a cottage are.

\*   \*   \*   \*   \*   \*

CAME soon the sturdy Mennonite
   From Russia's far-off shore;
Looked far around with wild delight
   And sought to roam no more;
For, this fair realm could realize
His wildest dreams of paradise!

Where his quaint structures dot the plain,
    He prunes the fruitful vine;—
Abodes of peace! Ah! not in vain
    Was crossed the treach'rous brine!
Here wealth awaits, 'tis his to seek
With land possessed in many a league.

Small need has he for civic courts;
    His calm, unruffled life,
The non-combative code supports,
    His creed forbidding strife.
Here conscience-favoring laws decree,
From war-like arts he shall be free.

# DEATH OF

# PRESIDENT LINCOLN.

# DEATH OF PRESIDENT LINCOLN.

WIDE o'er the land there comes a voice of wail!
    Why swells man's heart?—why woman's cheek
        so pale?
Dejected nature's gloomy shadow holds
The sombre earth draped in her pensive folds;
Sadly the night-winds whisper with a sigh
That name beloved, that name not borne to die!
A mighty name! to loyal hearts how dear?
'Tis one the traitor trembling dreads to hear.
Time's greatest nation mourns her chiefest pride,
And weeps convulsive for a friend and guide.—
Hark!—the slow knell that shakes the troubled air
With notes of woe, that tell of shroud and bier!—
The infant voice, the broken tones of age,
Shall pause to weep above the shrouded page.
Alas! his day too soon on earth was done;
Columbia weeps her greatest, noblest son.

Nor court intrigues e'er warped his love of truth,
Life's virtues claimed his manhood as his youth;
It ne'er was his the battle-blade to wield,
The senate called him louder than the field;
He swayed no scepter, and he wore no crown,
Though envious monarchs sought as high renown;
Greater than king who reigns above the slave,
Is chosen chief to guide the free and brave.

Through all thine acts a kindly nature shone;
The pardoned many mourn the statesman gone.
Like Amram's son to serfs thou freedom gave;
More abject than Old Egypt's Hebrew slave.
Scourged for long ages over Southern soil,
Groaning and bent to unrequited toil,
Nor bonds of kindred, woman's pleading tear,
Might sway the soul of tyrant overseer.
Long may the sons of Afric's sable race,
Shrined in each heart, give thy name deferend place.
Hot teeth of blood hounds now no more they fear;
Their clanking chains have ceased to larm the ear;
The lash has ceased dread tortures to prolong,
Sure vengeance finds the workers of their wrong.

The flag went down that shadowed o'er the hordes
That fled before the northern legion's swords:—

## DEATH OF PRESIDENT LINCOLN.

When wond'rous glory had the nation won,
When clouds had vanished from the nation's sun,
When were consigned to many an unknown grave,
Sons of the North, the valliant! the brave!
Staid was the hand of devastating war,
That spread destruction through the land afar;
Pealed the glad notes!—rejoicing bell was heard;—
"Peace!"—was the cry,—"A nation saved!" the word.
Alas! too soon, the loud-rejoicing bell
Was taught to toll the measure of a knell.

Cæsar victorious deemed his blood unsought
When Brutus robbed Rome by his damning plot.
Ambitious tyrants bearing haughty sway,
Oft'times with blood the price of crime do pay—
Could thou suspect?—How dared death's hideous mien
Lurk hungerly amid such brilliant scene?
Mirth in thine heart—gathered around thee there,
The capital's array of great and fair—
Ha! mark! a brow of lowering hate appear!
A spring!—a flash!—then gushed a people's tears.

That bold assassin did his work too well,
When thou, loved chieftain, mid thy glory fell.
Mid cruel griefs, foul wrongs so dark and deep,

Justice forbade her vengeance long to sleep.
Her blow has fallen, must thou fall alone,
When woe unutterable heard thy dying groan?

In Fame's proud temple still remains a niche
Besides the father of thy country, which
Throughout all time, thou, gen'rous soul, shall hold,
Thy name on high 'mong patriots enroll'd,
Who furious fought, intrepid, dauntless band,
Whose graves are green in freedom's smiling land;
Whose souls still watchful, hov'ring o'er the free,
Made thee their leader for posterity.

Shrined with the just, thy name shall never die!
The silent urn, where heroe's ashes lie,
May ne'er close o'er the mem'ry of the great,
While pean's praise shall sound thine high estate.
Though o'er the path of humbler life thou trod,
True genius raised thee from the grov'ling clod—
Emancipator! Savior of the slave!
Pil'd marble points a leader of the brave,
And Lincoln's name with Washington shall be
Revered while lives a nation of the free!
 EARLHAM COLLEGE, April 1865.

# THE SIEGE.

# THE SIEGE.

SHELLS, like demons wild, are shrieking through the
    thick and sulph'rous air,
In loud tones of terror speaking to the bold hearts
    gathered there.
Hostile ships are in the harbor, and the foe are on the
    land;
Loud the voice of war commingles with the waves upon
    the strand.

How the leaguered city echoes with the bursting
    bombshell's roar!
Far throughout its widest precincts fell destruction
    spreading o'er.
Mothers flee with wailing infants for some place of safety
    bound,
If, perchance, in that doomed city, refuge for the weak
    be found.

For, those wildly shrieking demons mercy show to man
 nor beast,
Like grim devils, hot from hades, here with death to hold
 a feast!

'Mid that scene of desperation, little heeding shot and
 shell—
Dealing death and devastation where the ruthless missiles fell;
'Mong the wounded and the dying, who are moaning
 round her there,
Woman's tenderest care supplying, moves a maid surpassing fair;
With a look of pity beaming from her classic features
 bright,
As a seraph's there descended from the boundless realms
 of light.
As she passes by their couches, wondering glances follow her;—
What kind power should send this angel who to them
 would minister?

Now, beside a couch she pauses, bending o'er a manly
 form;
Rupy lips have pressed his forehead, and she smoothes
 the temples warm;

Her sweet voice is like soft music, stealing on the
    dreamer's ear,
When the floating barque of Fancy bears the soul be-
    yond our sphere.
"Peaceful be thy slumbers, Ambrose, fiery fever's flush
    is gone,
And I hail thy growing vigor, as the sentinel the dawn."
   Then the warrior breathed low accents, when he found
    him not alone,
And perceived the eyes of beauty, beaming brightly in
    his own :—
"Dearest Ethel, thy sweet presence seems to herald
    health's return;
Soon the joyous tide of life shall bid no fevers fiercely
    burn—
Oh! those sunny days, dear Ethel, when the bloom of
    health is mine;
Oh! the city's joyous anthems, when the light of peace
    shall shine."

Darkly frowns the rocky fortress o'er the waters of
    the bay;
Lurid gleams flash from the vessels on the deep sea, far
    away;
Drearily break the waves of ocean, as her tide sweeps
    o'er the sand,

And the gloomy shades of nightfall spread their pall above the land.
Ominous silence waits upon the dreadful breaking forth of power,
For, the warlike hosts have ceased their dismal carnage for the hour.
Fondly looks the warrior lover on the maiden at his side,
Clasping Ethel's lily hand, soon destined for his loved and lovely bride!—
"But why lurks that shade of sadness 'neath the drooping lashes now?"
Then he smoothed the braids of amber, as he pressed the fair young brow.
"No! thou shalt not stay, my Ether; for thy safety much I fear,
Where destruction wide is spreading—where death's angel hovers near!
Though the morrow brings our marriage, when I claim thy hand as mine,
Would thou quit the city, Ethel, till the light of peace shall shine?"

Boldly spoke the peerless maiden:—"While the brave are falling near,

I will wed thee on the morrow, though my joy is blent
    with fear.
O'er my soul, last night, in dreaming, direful fancies
    round would hover,
When it seemed a demon bore me from the bosom of my
    lover!"
"Be not downcast, darling Ethel, let me see thee smile
    again.
When thou art my bride, to-morrow, we will both be
    happy then!"


As the restless waves are breaking hoarse along the
    sandy shore,—
Hark ye to the opening thunder!—'Tis the cannon's
    wrathful roar!
Oh! the dark tide of the future! whither does thy current
    bear?
Oh! to pierce the cloud of evils when its shadow draw-
    eth near!


Now the organ's swelling anthems rise and fall through
    dome and isle,
As the measured boom of cannon with its music blends
    the while!

Let the chapel portal open! for a bride divinely fair,
By her lover's arm supported, in her beauty enters there.

With her bridal robes as spotless as the virgin snows
of earth,
Flowing round her form, so fautless, seemeth she of
heavenly birth.
Lo! the youth who moves beside her, in his warlike
trappings bound,
Is a soldier from the battle, with his sword still girt
around!
That gay throng who follow after are a fair and goodly
train :—
Shall they all, who cross that threshold, in life's vigor
pass again?

Bridal robes mid scenes of carnage! death alone light
tones may hush.
Cupid's arrows are not idle, though life's ills arise to
crush.
Though pale horrors gather round her, love-light beams
in beauty's eye;
When the golden chain has bound her, Love, though
vanquished, cannot die.

In his sacred robes of office waits the priest to seal the
    bans,—
Ethel, Ambrose stand united by knit hearts and clasp
    of hands.
On his lips the word yet lingers—e'er the bride's re-
    sponse is given,
Comes the dreadful shrieking demon!—loud the frighted
    air is riven,
With the crashing of his thunder;—Wildest shrieks of
    terror rose,
Thrilling every sense with horror!—Lo! the lurid lights
    disclose,
Those in agony low writhing!—Ah! 'tis shocking to
    behold
The warm life-blood slowly ebbing from those loving
    hearts and bold.


As grim death with icy fingers touches lips once full of
    mirth,
And the glazing eye-light lingers for a last farewell of
    earth—
List! that moan—like zephyr sighing for the perished
    autumn day!
'Tis the dying wail of Ethel, who among the bleeding
    lay!

"Oh! thou shalt not perish, Ethel!" and her form the
    warrior raised;
Then upon the anguished features, long and earnestly
    he gazed:—
"Oh! my darling!—thou art yet mine!—oh! the icy
    hand of death!
Breathe, oh! breathe the word, my seraph, e'er thou
    draw thy latest breath."

Then unclosed the eye-lids softly, and the pale lips
    murmured "Yes,"—
While the bridegroom bending, o'er her, gave the parting
    bridal kiss;
For the life-blood fast is ebbing—now he feels the hand
    grow cold;
And she sleeps in death reposing, while his arms her form
    enfold.

On the morrow, fierce contending, Ambrose fell beside
    the wave,
And the maidens wove their chaplets over his and Ethel's
    grave;
Where magnolias shed sweet fragrance and the weeping
    willows grow,
When peace smiled upon the city, and the sullen foe
    withdrew.

# CHARGE OF THE

## ICONOCLAST.

# CHARGE OF THE ICONOCLAST.

### AN ALLEGORY.

HIS charger gleams white as the wild albatros,
    Fleet as the far meteor darting across,
  Caparisoned for the fierce fray;
Bedecked with bright stars, like the belt of Orion;
And his charge is resistless as that of the lion,
  When he springs through the night on the prey.

Like the foam of the ocean caught up from the seas,
The mane of the steed floats afar on the breeze
  From a neck arching grandly and proud;
His nostril, spread wide, snuffs the air from afar,
Alert for the terrible opening of war,
  And his voice like the thunder is loud!

The warrior who guides wears a countenance firm,
Each movement displaying his grandeur of form,
   In double-mailed garments of light.
But his look is benign, and his face is so fair,
Though the proud power of triumph looks forth in his
      air,
   Neath locks like the sable of night.

A giant's huge sledge at his saddle bow swings;
The broad shield is of gold, that behind him he slings,
   In shape like the disk of the moon;
While the rider and steed are illumined all o'er,
With a radiance that shines many leagues on before,
   And behind with the brightness of noon.

Either hand, like a wall, rises blackness of night,
Save where it is pierced by that vision of light,
   As fleet as the speed of the blast!—
Away! and away!—with a dart, and a flash!—
He heeds not the roar of the torrent's loud crash,
   As river and mountain are past.

On! onward he speeds!—If a mortal were nigh,
His spirit would quail neath the flame in that eye,
   As a city's proud spires rise in view!
'Tis the land of the East! where the radiant dome

Gives to myriads of priests a luxuriant home,
  Whose tythings augmented still grow.


The Iconoclast comes, heeding never their cry,
As the people fall prostrate, but, passing them by,
  The temple's proud portal he gains.
How he hurls the huge sledge with a ponderous power!
How the pagoda quakes from firm basement to tower,
  By the force of fierce shocks it sustains!


Bright legions appear at the sound of that blow!
Striving on till the temple's proud grandeur lay low—
  Transformed in an instant from light!
Then, the steed with his rider spring fleet through the
        air,
Nor an instant delay, while the myriads throng there,
  And the multitude scattered in flight.


From the ruins arose, where the temple had stood,
A structure full vast; and its cognomen, "GOOD",
  Was graven in adamant stone.
Then a rostrum arose where the idol had been,
And an Angel of Light taught the people therein
  Of Nature's God reigning alone.

The foe to false deities o'er the plain sped,
By flaming volcano and battle field red,
   Where the vintage rich treasures bestowed;
The huge hammer hurtled 'gainst many a shrine,
Where a kingdom was crushed in the land of the vine,
   And despots saw tyranny bowed.

Yet, the stern rider heard not the murmurs that came—
Devastation that swept with the torch's fierce flame—
   As he smote Superstition's high places;
For, the Legions of Light ever came at his call,
As he caused the proud structures of Error to Fall,
   Before the grim priests' pallid faces.

The opposing Pope rose!—quickly fled in affright!
As his minions grew blind in the glare of the light!
   While crashed their cathedral's proud altar.
As prone in the dust lay the Virgin and shrine,
Unheeded the bauble's auriferous shine
   By the firm and unfaltering assaulter.

That vast structure was found in Italia's fair clime,
Whose grandeur, far-reaching, high towered sublime
   Above Superstition's proud dome.
Then the architrave fell by great Angelo laid,

And the beautiful altar-piece, gorgeous arrayed,
  At the crash of St. Peter's at Rome!


But the Gods of the nations came not to oppose
The image-destroyer, nor yet the pale foes
  Of Darkness, Superstition and Error;
Whose toils are unceasing, who never give o'er
Till the foundations fall of the temples of yore,
  And joy takes the place of grim terror.


No structure so firm but comes down at a blow,
Spread wide on the plain, in crushed ruins below,
  When the pale rider smites with his sledge.
In the land of inquisitors monuments fall,
And delusions of spirit no longer appall,—
  Soul-freedom redeemeth the age!


All realms of the earth the pale charger speeds through,
And still her proud pinnacles sink from the view
  In the lands by the farthest seas!
That vast people flourishing—know as "The Free,"—
Whose gods are ten thousand—who bow low the knee—
  Are awaked from their lethargic ease.

For, the Legions of Light are abroad in that land
Where smites unrelenting the merciles hand,
  And the people give heed to their preaching;
Free rostrums arise where the images were,
O'er which the fair monuments splendid appear,
  Whose spires through the skies are far-reaching.

Men lighted huge fires with vast volumes of flame—
Hard pressed by the whirlwind the blinding smoke came,
  Far round in red fierceness they rolled!
And forests were felled to oppose the swift course
Of the rider who guided the mystic white horse,
  Whom barrier never controlled;

Whose course is unchecked though the earthquake is
    nigh,
And no idol he spares, though men's dogmas may die,
  Neither stays for refreshment nor rest;
For, his charger exists on the vapors which rise
From the gardens of earth where the white lilly dies,
  To obey the angelic behest.

Now the breaker of images speedeth away
Fulfilling his mission;—rides far to obey
  The myriads of ministering immortals;

And, although the earthquake, though vain man doth oppose,
Though the phalanx impregnable seemeth of foes,
They appear through the wide-open portals.

# MISCELLANEOUS.

*This descriptive poem forms the prelude to a tale in verse, entitled " The Maid of the Mississippi," soon to be published by the same author.*

*The poems to Tennyson and Bryant, which immediately follow, are selections from " A Tribute to the Poets," which will appear complete, in the same volume with the above mentioned tale.*

*See fly leaf at the end of this volume.*

# NIGHT SCENE ON THE MISSISSIPPI.

THE mystic moon's celestial sphere
    Rides on the broad expanse of wave,
Twixt mural mountains, frowning drear
Above the wandering Spaniard's grave;
On whose broad breast, like Maldive barque,
Reflected floats each starry spark.
Monarch of waters! wild and wide!
Dark, gloomy, depths of turbid tide!
Slow rolling on,—an endless sea,
Majestic, deep, perpetually.
Oh! wondrous tide of power, that flows
To tropic seas from Arctic snows!

Grim giants drive a deep-mouthed roar
From slimy depths of yawning caves,
Wave-washed within, well worn with waves,
Dark in the dim receeding shore.

The sluggish tributary's flow
From yonder shadowy defile
Sweeps slowly round the sedgy isle;
Swirling in shoals of crested snow,
Through prostrate, grasping arms of grey;
In bayou, marsh, and lagoon shallow,
Uncouth and grim in moon-light yellow,
The alligator waits his prey.

The myriad flocks at twilight glow
That lined the sands like drifting snow,—
The fisher-fowl have sought the fen,
That all day gleaned a livelihood
From tender bulb and finny brood,—
Diedipper, coot, and pelican.

Flow on! grand flood! whose wealth creates
From forests drear, fair, fruitful states;
Whose blooming vales e'erwhile were rife
With unrelenting civic strife.
Nor always borne, benignly mild
By slumb'ring shores with plenty blest,
Like tyrant with his wrath at rest,—
Destruction waits thy waters wild!

## NIGHT SCENE ON THE MISSISSIPPI.

Mad in thy myriad miles of might,
The darkly dreadful surges pour
A vasty deep o'er either shore,
Above the dyke's impotent height.
Man may not stay thy ruthless sway;—
Roaring in wrath through wide crevasse,
The raging, surging waters pass,
Whose force no power on earth shall stay!
Mid crashing trunks in swirling sweep,
The pale, grief-stricken planter yields
His fair plantation's feathery fields
To thy destruction, boundless deep!


Light-gliding birch canoes have flown
Where thy far northern waters lone,
Unstained by red Missouri's hue,
Sheeted in clearest glassy blue,
Lock arms with wild Saskatchawan.
But now the barques that cleave thy crest
A nation's wealth bear o'er thy breast.
Ages have passed; the wigwam stood
Where cities tower along thy flood,
And pour vast treasures toward that goal
Where warm the Mexic waters roll.

Along thy wave reach radiant beams
Which night's long loneliness have riven;
Glanced by the quiet queen of heaven,
Who rules our period of dreams.
She casts her diamonds down to dance
Amid the transitory band,
Like frolic elves from fairy land,
Over the river's broad expanse.

On such a night the starry wave
Became De Soto's silent grave.
He dared the ocean for this tomb;
Oh! sombre stream! whose name he gave,!
In many mighty marches came.
Not spectres of the dismal swamp,
Nor prowling Indian's deadly hate,
Nor panther howling round his camp
Revoked his desolating fate,
While threading wild or fording wave,
Till death took the intrepid brave.

The torch on high was flaming red,
While priest with flaming censer led
*Te Deum's* solemn anthem deep
Above the Spaniard's dreamless sleep;

In Castile's banner sadly wound,
With sword agrasp, by helmet crowned.

  Midway the dark sepulchral stream
They lowered the hero from their barque;
Above him closed the waters dark;
Down deep the lifeless burthen fell;
Came from the shore the panther's scream,
O'er rippling wave and lonely dell.
Then slowly veered the funeral barque
Toward the still shore-line, dim and dark—
Rowed in sad silence, lest the foe
His death and burial place should know.

# TENNYSON.

GREAT Tennyson! from Fame's high mountain brow,
    Canst hear my shell, so far off, faint and low,
That tribute sends o'er plain and ocean's flow?
The charm that plays along thy faultless line,
No mortal pen hath cunning to define;
Whose clust'ring gems in rare effulgence shine
Like diamonds pure from some prolific mine.
Through realms of beauty hath thy spirit stray'd,
Whose bloom profusive o'er thy verse is laid;
As when the maidens strew the floral shower
At hero's triumph in his glory's hour.

  Thy jewel lamp with glories of the day,
Illumines time with meteoric ray.
Astounded critics scan thy rythmic page,—
Thy matchless might bears thee beyond their rage!
What power is thine to charm this all-wise age?

Oh, lovely Maude! Oh, dreams of Locksley Hall!
Poor Enoch Arden! Princess! Idyls all!
Sad in Memorium! Golden Festival!—
The drama calls thee!—proud Queen Mary stands,
Cold, cruel, courtly—pale, with crimson hands,
While groaning martyrs burn through British lands;
Doomed Harold wars with Norman William's host,
Till crown and kingdom, hope and life are lost.
Behold! the Muse holds forth as thine award,
The mantle meet of Avon's deathless bard!

# BRYANT.

ILLUSTRIOUS Bryant! patriarchal bard!
    Rejoicing nature varied language heard
When thy pure harp amid her solitudes,
Chanted the glories of her changeful moods;
Hymning thy praise, tuned to the sighing bough,
Where scented air of meadows cools thy brow;
Vast prospects wake thy contemplative mood,
And bid the picture lakelet, stream and wood;
The humming-bird, that sports amid the spray;
The water-fowl, that cleaves the airy way;
The green bank, dinted by the timid deer;
The wolf that laps, the growling slow-paced bear.

  No fierce convulsions jar thy life's smooth flow,
Nor penury brings scenes of want and woe.
Though oft rare genius hath its ray obscured,
In attic dim, by poverty immured,

Fair fortune o'er thee spread a lavish hand,
Though thy pure life wealth's luxury disdain'd.
Fame's proud exaltings worked no change in thee,
Sage of a nation's sweetest minstrelsy!
Dear to the children of thy native land,
Linked with her loveliest scenes thy name shall stand.

# UNREST.

YE evening winds that gently blow,
    And soft on balmy pinions bear,
Haste ye to breathe where flow'rets grow,
    To feast amid their fragrance rare?
Ye lately mourned for they who died,
    Your sweet companions of the plain—
Would ye they might for aye abide?
    Alas! the chilling blasts have slain.

Why do ye sigh, oh! gentle winds!
    While floating o'er the brightest scenes?—
"The gayest grot bleak sorrow finds,
    Twixt hope and joy grief intervenes."
Soft, unseen mourners, why should ye
    Seem sorrowing o'er my absent joys?
And with me murmur, "Woe is me!"
    Sighing that care man's peace destroys?

While whispering o'er this vernal sphere,
  Find ye no spot that ever shines?
Where naught is dampt by briny tear,
  Where the glad bosom ne'er repines?
Have ye ne'er sought those joyous bowers,
  Where love reclines that poets sing?
Where sylphs delight the honied hours,
  And naught may hush the lute's light string?

Where ne'er beside the banquet board,
  O'er his divan the monarch sees,
By brittle hair, the gleaming sword
  Suspended o'er his couch of ease?
What do I hear?—an answering sigh,
  Responsive to my query bold,
Oh! listen to the sad reply:—
  "Peace ne'er abode with mortal mould."

# GEESE.

OF all the domestic fowls fit for man's use,
    For down or for roasting, the best is the goose;
And although the roast turkey, a dish of renown,
At Christmas much talked of in country and town,
May be savory, indeed, yet were we to compare
The goose with the turkey, we could but declare
That the preference, indeed, to the former were due,
To be ever chosen by epicure true.—

  Prepared by the garcon for *table 'd hote*,
As a dish for excelling the fillagreed shoat,
Have the dressing with spices appropriately mix'd,
And the fowl on the salver attactively fix'd—
Just browned to a crisp, while the fragrant sauce flows,
Nicely seasoned, betwixt the potatoes in rows;
Then glorious, indeed, are the odors which rise,
E'en tempting the gods from their feast in the skies.

Artistically carve now, with consummate art,
To each guest expectant dispose of a part;
Send orders for desert, and serve on the wine—
Oh! who could the joys of such feasting resign?
We are of the earth earthy, and appetite craves
The good things of life; yet, when Gluttony's slaves
Bow low to her mandates, with scarcely a doubt,
They are held on the rack by Dyspepsia and Gout.

Who has not at evening reposed with his head
On light, downy pillow while weariness fled?
But who finds for pity a place in his mind,
Or feels for the woes or the goose and its kind?
For, oh! it is doleful while plucking the geese,
And rending the delicate, snowy-white fleece,
To list to the heart-rending clamor they raise,
But the pityless picker her hand never stays;
For, a daughter will soon to the altar be led,
And the matron, of course, must present her a bed!
Then, soft as the thistle down wafted on high,
Is the couch whereon rosy young beauty shall lie.

When the geese are plucked nakedly ragged and lean,
Realizeing that they are unfit to be seen
Divest of their plumage—dejected and drooping,
How touching the scene is? as o'er the lawn trooping,

And striving to hide from the eye their disgrace,
They seek in the woodland a safe hiding place?
Instinctively shrinking from view in their pain,
Till nature symmetrically clothes them again.
Then, how graceful the geese! as in squadrons they sail
O'er the clear, glassy lake in their plumage so pale;
Where, steering and veering, their feathers they lave,
And dive in their frolics beneath the bright wave.

When Rome was at war with a neighboring state,
The foe were in ambuscade lying in wait ;
And seeking by stratagem, thus to beguile
The Romans to march through a narrow defile ;
Then a flock of geese passed where the enemy lay,
Loud clamoring with fright in a terrible way;
So the legions were warned, when they would have
        passed in,
And the foe were disgusted, and left in chagrin.
Thus Rome was preserved by the gabbling of geese,
And their flocks were protected and 'lowed to increase.

By-the-way, of the goose many species are known,
And the rivers out west by wild flocks are o'erflown—
Nor always distinguished by feathers alone;
For, a goose may wear broad-cloth, fine boots, and a hat,
Sport a cane, a cigar, moustache and all that—

Howbeit, this species dishonors the bird,
Although of the fowl they may claim to be lord;—
And noted for thinking their crests higher by far,
Than, truthfully speaking, they actually are;
For, a goose upon passing an entrance will nod,
Though the opening above may extend a full rod.

A goose by the tailor is oft in request,
By means of which seam and lappel are impressed;
When tooth-picks are needed, the biped again
Appears as a valued assistant to men;
With the quill of the goose, e'er usurped by the steel,
The author his thoughts to the world would reveal;
And well might the writer of that day concede
That the plume of this bird was a blessing, indeed.

Of this biped a story is wont to be told
With an excellent moral, although it be old;
To the doings of men it will aptly apply,
And a hint of such value should never go by.

There dwelt an old woman—I cannot tell where—
And a goose she possessed with this attribute rare;
For, instead of producing, to nature so true,
Such eggs as 'tis known that all other geese do,
To believe in the truth of the story as told,

You must think that the eggs of this bird were of gold!
The ancients had said, 'twas a gift from the gods!
Who cares how she got it?—a fig for the odds!

The lugubrious owner, by valuable lays,
Was quickly enabled 'bove neighbors to raise;
But, as weak human nature is seldom, if ever,
Satisfied with enough, so she now must endeavor
To possess all the gold of the wonderful goose,
Though for it she found no immediate use;
'Twas avarice that caused her to seek as she did,
And to carve for the eggs where she thought they were
  hid.

She laid open the goose with a horn-handled knife,
Which, as naturally followed, deprived it of life;
Then who can imagine her grief and surprise,
When never an egg met the old woman's eyes!
But, alas! for the fowl which had brought her such gain,
With covetous hand she had ruthlessly slain;
Then the old woman's fortunes grew rapidly worse,
Till poverty came with a terrible curse.
Thus, the moral is very explicitly shown:—
We are wise to let well enough ever alone.

# THE HAUNTED SOUL.

YES, 'tis past!—those ties are severed,
    Which have held thine image near;—
Unforgotten! heartstrings quivered
    O'er remembrances so dear!

Years those tender ties have bound me,
    But the cords are snapt for aye,
And when lovely forms surround me,
    Shall I think on thee away?

I remember how I met thee
    In my youth's too balmy spring;—
How I've striven to forget thee,
    While my heart was withering!

Now those sunny days are over;—
    Happy dreams! too sweet to last!

And their mem'ries deep I cover,
    Sleeping with the buried past.

I have feasted on remembrance,
    And my soul has queried then,
If thy form of beauty's semblance
    I should ever clasp again?—

Let his store of gold controll thee!
    Better far than love or grace;
'Tis the thought that shall console me;—
    Perish heart that holds it base!

Yet, I find no voice to censure;
    Now my heart grows never chill;—
What were I, that I should venture
    To a place that gold should fill!

Aye! though Fortune smile upon thee,
    Ostentation be thine own,
All the sweets of love will shun thee—
    Gold hath taken wings and flown!

Yes! I know thy love is fickle,
    And thy smiles are cheaply bought.

## THE HAUNTED SOUL.   155

Now, perchance, thou'lt reck but little—
   Time and anguish waken thought.

Though thy fond looks greet another,
   Still his blissful dream is short;
Though the hands be clasped together,
   Love alone secures the heart.

Cold indifference breeds dissention;
   Then the yawning gulf appears,
Still unbridged by good intention;—
   Oh! the floods of scalding tears!

He may greet thee fondly, kindly,
   Dreaming of his treasure won;
Thou wilt smile upon him blandly,
   When thy soul shall seek to shun.

And the bitter words, reproving,
   Lightly slumbering, soon shall wake;
Then the cold heart, still unloving,
   In its lonely tomb shall ache.

When the silent tear shall wander
   O'er that cheek once beauty's throne,

Then thou may'st in silence ponder,
  O'er the love forever flown.

Gaul hath usurped all life's sweetness;
  Where 'twas brightest, gloom appears;
Once, the moment's wings had fleetness;
  Now, how wearily drag the years?

All the hopes of life are blasted;—
  How their ghosts wail on the blast!
Joys which might through time have lasted,
  Down Oblivion's waters past.

But my soul awakes from dreaming
  O'er mutations brought by time;—
Wide's the world, with beauty teeming,
  Calling loud to deeds sublime!

# THE FESTIVAL FILLS ME WITH SADNESS.

THE festival fills me with sadness,
   Though light be the strains that I hear;
Sweet music which woke me to gladness,
   Now moistens mine eye with a tear.

Within the gay circle I'm lonely,
   Though beauty's fond smiles I may see;
I am moved with one thought of thee only!
   Oh! think'st thou, sweet Florence, of me?

From every loved spot I am staying,
   Which we by our wanderings endeared;
Suppressing the deep sigh betraying,
   The heart that a sorrow has seared.

Oh! is there no semblance of feeling
  Thy bosom may cherish e'en yet?
A thought that thine heart is concealing?
  A something akin to regret?

False! false to the bosom that cherished
  Thy beautiful image in vain!
The heart that for thee would have perished,
  Oh! was it thy pleasure to pain?

Where beauty and youth are assembling,
  I drive retrospection away;
For, why should I dream that dissembling
  Dwells with such fair creatures as they?

Yet, he whom that sunny glance blesses,
  May feel his fond cheek to grow pale;
And learn that soft looks and caresses
  May all in their tenderness fail.

Though her beautiful cheek be as roses,
  Her brow than the lily more fair,
In that jeweled bosom reposes,
  Deceipts and a treacherous snare.

# THE SOUL'S MIRROR.*

FAIR woman's heart sustains within
    A voice to prophesy akin;
A wail of warning, vaguely sent;
    More clear her far-divining eye
    Than subtlest man's philosophy.
Mysterious presentiment!
That would the way for woe prepare,
Or life's rude shocks could illy bear
Her gentler nature, frail as fair.

The heart may close its portals all;
Still glares that visage o'er the wall,
Where sits the scowl of sullen fate
That ceaseless clamors at the gate.

*From "The Maid of the Mississippi,"—a tale in verse, soon to be issued by the same author.

Oh! there is naught the heart can melt
  Like beauty troubled; naught relieving
Her poignant pangs of anguish felt—
  More lovely in her silent grieving;
When sculptured lips no word essay
To tell what hides their smile away;
Like shadow stealing o'er the flower,
The lingering shade of gentlest shower;
Intensyfying every grace
Exquisite on the lovely face;
Where soul seems mounting to those eyes
In whose depths nameless magic lies.


As white frost fades before the gleam
Of early morn's approaching beam,
Speeds that cold barrier, ever wound
So closely stranger hearts around;
For, that strange spell is o'er us thrown
That binds the soul beside its own;
In sublimated essence shrined,
Two spirits blending as one mind;
Then thoughts well up within the breast
That seem to inward ears addressed;
Their soft import conveyed to each
Without the form of outward speech;

Should murmuring lips low tones diffuse,
Let not the ear an accent loose.

Earth brings from heaven its chiefest charm,
To beautify the fautless form,
Whose lines shall be immortal;—never
   Is rosy-tinted beauty lost;
Returning there to live forever,
   Beyond time's treacherous ocean tost;
Unmared by sorrow, gloom or care,
To beam perpetually there.

## TO H \* \* \* \* \*.

---

OH! would'st thou ask a line of me
   To breathe my faithful heart's devotion?
Dear one! my life is lived for thee;
   Thy smile or tear shades each emotion.

I saw thy face—changed grew the world!
   I dreamed not of the pending danger;
Misfortune's cruel darts were hurled, .
   And peace was to my soul a stranger.

Oh! then I only lived to sigh;
   My hopes and-joys all fled together;
Each pleasure passed unheeded by,
   And clouds of gloom hung low to smother.

Oh! thou may never, never doubt,
   This heart, which nought hath power of changing;

Still loving, constant, while about,
   The fires of sullen fate are raging.

I loved thee for thy woman's soul
   And won the fond, the precious treasure;
Resigning to thy light control
   Devotion nought can ever measure.

I knew that thou wert pure and fair;
   Ideal of my heart resembling:—
My Muse lacks language to declare
   What made me thine without dissembling.

And it shall ever be my part,
   To strive for what to thee is pleasing;
To know no sorrow sears thine heart,
   To make thine happiness unceasing.

Each earthly grief shall loose its sting
   When I may see my Hattie smiling;
For thou, dear one, the balm may bring
   The sadest hour of grief beguiling.

# OH GENTLY BLOW, YE AUTUMN GALES.

*A SONG.*

OH! gently blow the autumn gales,
    Where flowrets bloom the rarest;
Of maids that roam Miami's vales,
    My Fanny was the fairest.

Her hair in many a golden band,
    O'er cheeks as roses blooming,
Was braided by her gentle hand,
    The lilly's hue assuming.

Beside Miami's waters bright,
   That at our feet were flowing,
We gazed upon the ripples light,
   And felt the breezes blowing.

Oh! tender were the words we said,
   Beside that lovely river;
Although her sunny smiles are fled,
   My Fanny lives forever.

# REMORSE.

WHO can conceive so dire a hell
    As rages in the human breast,
For her entombed who loved thee well,
    Whose presence like an Angel's blessed?
Whose wounded soul too deeply felt
The blow thy deed of madness dealt?
Neglect, thy madly reckless course,
Drove daggers home with deadly force;
Then, of thy flower of beauty shorn,
Thou'rt left in solitude to mourn.

    Remorseful pangs, like lava, roll
Their seething billows o'er the soul;
And in their track rush frantic there,
Pale horror, anguish, and despair.
Remorse! thou hast a fearful sting!

Reason may no consoling bring
To this life woe, so withering.

Hope blighting as the upas shade
That shadows Knifon's tainted glade;
Alas! from thee is no return;
Still thine unslumb'ring fires burn,
And the seared heart forever cries,
Stung barbed scorpions till she dies.

# YOUR SISTER.

WHO found you when young,
    Where the peaches were hung
From a pin in the wall of the kitchen?
    And when you ne'er thought
    In the theft to be caught,
Your labor repaid with a switchin'?
          Your sister.

When the tea-table smoked,
    And when you became choked,
Who begun 'twixt your shoulders a-pounding?
    And stopped all your cries
    For cakes and for pies,
By the doctrines of hygiene expounding?
          Your sister.

While speeding away,
    The inverted sleigh

With the shafts and the timbers went crashing:—
   Who was it who sat
   On your new beaver hat
As into the snow you went dashing?
         Your sister.

   Who was it you led
   On the log o'er the bed
Of the stream which below you went dashing?
   Who sliped from your hold,
   And after you rolled
Into the cold stream with a splashing?
         Your sister.

   And who was the lass,
   When you sat in the class,
Kept your mind from its task ever breaking?
   And drawing your looks
   Far away from your books,
Would keep your poor heart ever acheing?
         Somebody else's sister!

# SHE LIVES AGAIN.

OH! dost thou know a power on high
    With every grace has blessed thee?
Then marvel not, sweet maid, that I
    A wanderer, addressed thee.

Thou hast the faultless form of one,
    Whose memory I cherish;
Whose fleeting day too soon was done,
    And she, alas! must perish.

For, Oh! she faded,—I was left
    In this false world, so lonely;
I roam afar, because bereft
    Of her I lived for only.

Her spirit shone with every grace,
    Sweet purity could render;

None e'er might look upon her face
    Nor feel his soul grow tender.

And when thy father's brilliant hall
    On that bright eve I entered,
When hearkened all to pleasure's call,
    My gaze on thee was centred.

I saw upon thy features play
    The smile that beamed so sweetly;
So loved by me in that bright day
    That passed away too fleetly.

Thy sparkling eye, thy raven hair,
    Alike were her possession;
The rosy lips, and brow so fair,
    And thine the same expression.

And when my glance dwelt on thee then,
    I felt my heart grow lighter;
It seemed she was on earth again,
    And I, once more, beside her.

# EARLHAM COLLEGE GAMES.

SHALL Earlham's day remain unsung,
    And find no voice to sing its praise?
For love and war loud harps have rung;
    Bards to the bowl pour deathless lays!

One faithful harp shall praise thy games;
    One bard shall sing with greatful heart!
The Muse shall ne'er reject thy claims,
    Till memory and youth depart!

Olympic games the Grecians had,
    And widely far was spread their fame;
In ancient day his heart was glad
    Whose prowess won the festive game.

Vain Nero played at chariot race,
    With heroes strove the prize to gain;

And from their thrones, in pride of place,
    Kings cheered the coursers o'er the plain.

Would we renounce our gladsome play
    For one that early Greece possessed?
When gods and games have passed away—
    On classic page alone exist?

How fondly dear the cherished hour
    Which we in field-sport pleasures spent?
When life's deep shadows round us lower
    To be with storm and tempest blent?

Ah! well we loved the lively game,
    The wild excitement of the play!
Which bade to scorn the slothful name,
    And fleetly speed the ball away!

'Mid intervals from toil apart,
    When loosed from Locke, from Virgil free,
What rapture thrilled each youthful heart!
    How rang the air with frolic glee!

The chieftains brave arrayed their sides,
    With dauntless mien,—as heroes are;

And when the ball so swiftly rides,
  Begins the surging tug of war!

As though engaged in martial strife—
  The contest urged with might and main—
Though seeking no opponent's life,
  Oft lies he prostrate on the plain.

And when the swiftly fleeting ball,
  Propelled by many a sturdy blow,
Eventfully hath reached the goal,
  The victors' wild exultings flow!

Oh! regaljoust! forever live,
  When I thy praises sing no more!
On Earlham's grounds benignly thrive,
  While life's mad maelstroms round me roar!

EARLHAM COLLEGE, 1864.

# THE AUCTIONEER.

WHILE passing one evening up Madison street,
    A flaming red flag chanced my vision to greet;
And painted in letters, at least a yard long,
The word I beheld there which now heads my song.
A bell was kept vigorously gingling the while,
The multitude passing within to beguile.

As the protent word, "AUCTION," appeared to
    my sight,
I read the bill over beside the gas light;
While I stood there perusing the huge-lettered bill,
I heard a voice yelling both loudly and shrill,
"How much am I offered?" and, "Going at ten!"
The words were repeated again and again.

Curiosity prompted to enter and see
What caused such a shouting—such ardour and glee.—
To answer his query, "How much am I bid?"
Within 'mong the bidders I shortly was hid.


On a box stood a man who in statue was small,
His shadow reflected behind on the wall;
He swayed his arms wildly, straining hard at his throat,
Quite freely perspiring, divest of a coat;
His round face was ruddy, his nose, too, was read,
And hair the same color lay thick o'er his head.
How the laugh of his hearers rang loudly and shrill
At the jokes which he cracked with a hearty good will!


"How much am I offered?"—repeating his cry,
As he a huge rocking-chair brandished on high:—
"I pid you von dollar vor dot rocking-chair!"
A provident dutchman replied to him there—
"Och! an' two dollars I'll bid ye for that!"
Responded the liberal Irishman, Pat.
"Now, going! still going!—who gives me the half?"
His words became witty, and raised a loud laugh.
"Still going!—and going!—the sturdy voice rang—
And sold!—as the hammer came down with a bang!"

## THE AUCTIONEER. 179

The contest was ended; Pat shouldered the chair,
And moved through the crowd with his prize in the air;
For the place was well peopled with boys, and with men,
A few came to purchase, while others again,
Came to hear the man joke, who so loudly did yell,
And whose words were rolled forth with tremendous
      swell.

"How much am I offered?" the auctioneer cried;
And the tones of his voice had the thunders defied,
As he held a split rolling-pin high in the air,
Menacingly flourishing over them there.
"Twenty cents!" said a by-stander, blinking his eyes,
As though he already had hold of the prize.
The party who bid wore a tall beaver hat,
Which, indeed, was quite seedy, and dinted at that.

A lean-visaged customer called, "Twenty-five!"
"That is a cheap rolling-pin, as I'm alive;"
The auctioneer said, as he handed the pin,
To the one who had bought it, with visage so thin.
Quite satisfied, too, then the man did appear,
For his wife had plead with him for more than a year,
To purchase an article like to the same,
Which he neath his arm now bore home to his dame.

The next thing the auctioneer showed to the crowd,
And he truly with sole-leather lungs was endowed,
Was a dozen of plates; some of them were cracked;
But the man well made up for that which they lacked,
By the praises thick lavished upon the said plates;
And offered to sell them, though some were not mates,
To the one who bid highest; and then he threw in,
To make them sell better, some platters of tin;—
Then bellowed such praises with ranting and roar,
As, I think I say truly, I ne'er heard before.

Old shoe-brushes, breast-pins, gold lockets and rules;
Together with hatchets, and all sorts of tools;
Hard-soap and dried-apples, and tables and chairs,
Surcingles, trunks, tooth-picks, keen razors, dull knives;
Big bread-bowls and wash-tubs, men bought for their
  wives.

A by-stander purchased a huge, yellow watch;
Broad dialect proved him undoubtedly Scotch—
Quickly paid for his treasure, passed out through the door,
And I'll warrant that auctioneer sold him no more;
For he thought of a truth 'twas a gold watch he had,
When truly the sharper had swindled him bad.

It chanced the Highlander while moving up street,
An honest acquaintance there happened to meet;
His good fortune disclosed to his friend's wond'ring eyes,
Jamie in raptures proclaimed—" A rich prize!"
He drew from his pocket the watch which did shine
As bright as the gold that is dug from the mine.—
" Ten dollars is all that I gave for the same!
As tr-r-uly I say it as Jamie's my name!
And almost I'd thought that the fellow had stole it,
Or he ne'er so cheaply to me would have sold it."—
Then the honest man found, to his sorrow, alas!
That the watch would not run, and that it was—*brass.*

## TO LEONA.

THE long years are fleeting, are going forever,
    No more to return with their pleasures and pains;
I ne'er can forget thee—how vain the endeavor?
    While life in this bosom its current maintains.

Forget thee! oh! never!—those orbs above shining,
    May cease to cheer earth with their radiance bright;—
Where thou art forgotten 'tis nought but repining,
    For thou art the star that still lendeth me light.

Thine image remaineth forever before me,
    As when thy companion through years that are gone;—
Oh! radiant Leona! deep sadness steals o'er me
    With dreams of the maiden of life's early morn.

How ripened our friendship to fond adoration!
    This heart poured its treasures at beauty's fair shrine;

I gazed on my idol with love's admiration;—
   My soul with fond rapture was bound up in thine.

The shadows of twilight at eve would decoy us,
   When moon-light was gladdening the gloom of the
      grove.
Oh! bliss ruled the hour! as unspeakably joyous
   As moon-beams light dancing on foilage above.

Oh! cruel the fortune our souls to so sever!
   Dark doom hath decreed each delight to conceal;
How useless the striving! soul grieve on forever,
   Subdued by the sorrow fate calls thee to feel.

# THE POACHERS' DEFEAT.

IN the midst of the night,
    When the lightning was bright,
We met at the cave in the valley;
    And, never delayed,
    By the storm dismayed,
To the rendezvous boldly did rally.

    Bold outlaws expelled,
    Grim want had impelled
To plunder to-night, the rich region;
    And should it be found
    That robbers were round,
We must flee, for the foemen were legion.

    E'er an hour had gone past,
    We beheld him at last,—
Our chief, we so anxiously waited;—

How vivid that flash?
And there followed a crash!
As the wrath of the storm culminated.

By the cavern without,
There rose a wild shout!
Could it be the dread foe were appearing?
We presently knew
The surmise untrue,
Nor heeded the tempest's careering.

Yet, again there arose
From friends or from foes,
For we recked not from which, such a clatter,
That, fearful of harm,
We sprang in alarm
To ascertain what was the matter!

From the cavern's rude door,
The torch flickered o'er
The countenance of Erin's fair daughter;
In affright did she fret,
As she shook off the wet,
Like a fowl just emerging from water.

"Hunt for Mikey," she said,
"I'm afraid he is dead!"
"Shure, his driving was nothing to brag on!
He has strayed from the road,
"An' mesilf has been throw'd
"On the horses' heels out of the wagon!"

By the light of the lamp,
Saturated with damp,
We beheld the lost traveler benighted;
Yet, we found him not killed,
Though potatoes were spilled,
And his lady was grieviously 'frighted.

"Och! Mikey, me dear!
"Where's the keg wid the beer?"
Were the first words by Bridget there spoken;
Whose feminine voice
Began to rejoice,
When none of Mike's bones were found broken.

They were guided again
From the dangerous plain,
To the road, where they thanked us full gladly.

As the night did prevail,
We secured all the ale,
Which had *treated* poor Mikey so badly!

Those benevolent men,
My companions, did then,
Unheeding the words of my warning,
Deeply drink of the draught;
And the ale which they quaffed,
O'ercame them with slumber till morning.

And the raid which was planned
By our valliant band,
That carousal at midnight defeated;
For the foe ascertained,
The marauders remained,
And, hotly persued, we retreated!

## TO MISS A * * * * B * * * * *.

---

FAIR-haired and graceful!—who can view
    Thy soft step by the foot-light fall,
Pressed lightly as the silver dew,
    But must some fairy scene recall?
The look that beams from thy sweet face,
    The sparkle dancing in thine eye,
That fautless form of moulded grace,
    The thousand charms that round thee lie!—

Oh! mistress of celestial chimes!
    There is a power vouchsafed to thee,
That bids thee bear through earthly climes
    Divinest strains of rhapsody.
For, from thy soft-toned silvery bells,
    Such notes are borne as angels hear!

And when their voice in sweetness swells,
   What rapture thrills the listening ear?


In harmony thine earliest thought
   Was cradled; while thine infant hand
To weave the tuneful arts was taught
   Which spell-bound thousands may command!
And, oh! what varied scene has been
   This changeful life to such as thou,
Who, with its lights, dark gloom has seen?
   Bright is the beam around thee now.


True genius brings thee fame, sweet maid!
   A people know thy power to charm;
With all thy matchless skill displayed,
   What heart but must grow fond and warm?
Never in former years has come
   So fair a charmer, skilled to bring
Such rare celestial music from
   The courts whose chimers the seraphs ring.


When those sweet bells, with tuneful tongue,
   Respond in pleasing gleeful notes,
While thy fair fingers dance among
   The chimes with the silver throats;

## TO MISS A * * * * B * * * * *.

Or when the horn would sound for thee—
  Its fair young mistress—who so well
Can wake its voice of melody,
  Delight lives in the magic spell!

# The Maid of the Mississippi,

A POETICAL ROMANCE OF THE RIVER,

BY

## THEODORE F. PRICE,

Is now ready for the press, and will soon be issued in elegant style, and beautiful binding: a companion volume to SONGS OF THE SOUTHWEST.*

---

What BAYARD TAYLOR, the celebrated traveler, author and poet says of it:

The author has just shown me the manuscript of "THE MAID OF THE MISSISSIPPI," a really beautiful poetical tale; I discover it to be highly meritorious. A vein of originality pervades it, and it contains some new and striking poetical features. The action is highly dramatic. There are four leading characters, strongly drawn; and the interest grows till the plot culminates. He informs me that he is in search of a publisher. I trust he will be successful, as there exists no work of like character.

TREMONT HOUSE, CHICAGO, 1875.

---

BENJ. F. TAYLOR, author of "Songs of Yesterday," "Sheaves of Rhyme," Etc., says:

"There is very decided dramatic and descriptive power in "THE MAID OF THE MISSISSIPPI," and the interest is admirably sustained. It ought to win the author golden opinions, and, if suitably produced, undoubtedly will."

---

WED. WILDER, author of "The Annals of Kansas," in Leavenworth, (Kas.,) *Times*:

"We have had the pleasure of reading the manuscript of a poem entitled "THE MAID OF THE MISSISSIPPI," by Theodore F. Price, and we have found every page sparkling with the unmistakable marks of the highest genius. The plot is simple, but not so simple as Alexander Smith's "Life Dream," so widely known in this country and Europe a few years ago. There is first a fine poetical description of our great river so dear to us of the West; and then we are taken on board a Mississippi steamer, a place hitherto unvisited by the poetic Muse, and events of one night are made to pass before our eyes with startling rapidity. Those who have spent a night upon the river, (and who in the West has not?) will readily accord to Mr. Price descriptive powers almost unequalled, as well as a wonderfully fine imagination, and taste of no common order. His characters stand out in bold relief, and preserve their characteristics distinct throughout the action of the whole story. His style resembles that of Shelly somewhat, although his poetry conveys a stronger human interest, characterized by remarkable vigor.

*SONGS OF THE SOUTHWEST will be forwarded on receipt of One Dollar.

Address, THEODORE F. PRICE, Wichita, Kansas.

www.ingramcontent.com/pod-product-compliance
Lightning Source LLC
Chambersburg PA
CBHW020934230426
43666CB00008B/1671